How to Make
MONEY
from
TRAVEL WRITING

Other books by Curtis Casewit:

Freelance Writing: Advice from the Pros
Freelance Photography
Making a Living in the Fine Arts
Colorado: Off the Beaten Path
Fodor's Colorado
Fodor's the Rockies (co-author)
Skiing Colorado
How to Get a Job Overseas
The Mountain World
Curtis Casewit's Guide to Tennis Resorts
The Literary Guide to the United States (co-author)

How to Make
MONEY
from
TRAVEL WRITING

by Curtis Casewit

The Globe Pequot Press

CHESTER, CONNECTICUT

Library of Congress Cataloging-in-Publication Data

Casewit, Curtis W.
    How to make money from travel writing / by Curtis Casewit.—1st
   ed.
          p.   cm.
    Bibliography: p.
    Includes index.
    ISBN 0-87106-668-8
    1. Travel—Authorship.   I. Title.
G151.C374 1988
808'.06691—dc19   88-16379
                                            CIP

Manufactured in the United States of America
First Edition / First Printing

Contents

Acknowledgments

I would like to thank Dave Smith of Winter Park's Hi Country Haus Resort, which is heaven for writers; Tina Harris, Beaver Village Condos; Mike Dybicz, manager of the Fraser Valley's best rental properties; Lillian Ross, the Keystone Four Season Resort; and the Antlers-at-Vail, where Rob LeVine and Bert Farin showed frequent hospitality. Continental Airlines enabled me to interview a great number of people for this book. I'm especially grateful to two of my colleagues, Steve Cohen and Randy Mink, for their advice. Last, the project would have been impossible without the help of Cecilia Caso, my assistant.

1

Ah, to Be a Travel Writer!

Travel Writing: A Distinguished Heritage

Ah, to be a travel writer! You are following in the footsteps of illustrious voyagers. Begin with the *Odyssey* and the wanderings of Odysseus; move through the centuries with diary-keeping Greek and Portuguese sailors and Mongolian military authors; explore with Christopher Columbus, in the service of Spain, and set foot on a Bahamian island; think of Marco Polo, the Venetian, climbing the far-flung Hindu Kush range and visiting what is now Beijing.

What a heritage! Consider essayist Henry David Thoreau taking his trip to Walden Pond, where he found himself "in the midst of pine and oakwood"; John Wesley Powell on the Colorado River, surrounded "by terraces of rock and tables of rock and rock everywhere"; Lewis and Clark, army officers, explorers and diarists, pushing west along the Missouri, the Snake and the Columbia rivers to the Pacific, cataloguing their travel adventures.

The present-day travel journalist seldom has to cope with the hardships—or at least discomforts—of preceding generations: Imagine Roald Amundsen and other explorers freezing at the South Pole, or French author Gustave Flaubert sweating in Egypt. By contrast, Henry James enjoyed his tour of France and raved about English horse races; Johann Wolfgang von Goethe sang the praises of Italy, "the land where the lemon trees bloom and the gold orange glows. . . . "

Is nature writing travel writing, too? For our purpose it could be. The width and breadth of the field allows for the outdoor descriptions of a John Muir hiking in the Sierras, a Ralph Waldo Emerson setting out into the Massachusetts forests, and an Annie Dillard observing Virginia's Blue Ridge country.

Many important authors leave home to tell us about the experiences in their own or other countries. Nobel Laureate John Steinbeck comes to mind: His *Travels with Charley* records his 10,000-mile, thirty-four-state journey in a pickup, with only his dog for company. Steinbeck's observations (especially of the Midwest) are keen; his writing flows so naturally, interestingly and beautifully that the book is worth reading more than once.

William Faulkner was asked to contribute to the (then literary) *Holiday Magazine* and Truman Capote traveled to North Africa for *Vogue*. Surely, Hemingway, writing in Spain, Cuba, Idaho, France and the Caribbean, produced not only novels but travel prose as well.

Currently the best travel journalism is often *literature.* The best practitioners seldom write for newspapers but for magazines and books. Examples? Paul Theroux has composed articles and longer works on Kampala, Singapore, New York, London and one hundred places in between; his *Great Railway Bazaar* and *Old Patagonian Express* or his many roadside essays are considered superior. Or read Kate Simon, a *literateuse* whose books about Rome, Siena and Vienna remain masterpieces.

During the last twenty years, some superb travel writing has become available. Consider Paul Bowles's stories about Morocco, Graham Greene on Haiti, Edna O'Brian on Ireland, John McPhee on Alaska, Hunter Thompson on Colombia. All give us eloquent examples of what the landscape and the local people are really like. All should serve as inspiration to the new travel journalist.

Varieties of Experience

Travel writing gives you an enormous variety of experiences. This chance to satisfy so many different urges can hardly be found in other types of journalism. To wit: One week, you experience the lovely voices of opera singers, the powers of symphony and piano concerti at a music festival in the Carolinas; the next week, you head southwest to Arizona to participate in a renowned arduous tennis clinic; and still on another Monday, you re-visit and report on Montana's Glacier National Park. If I look at all my published stories produced during one typical year, the variety of subjects seems staggering. That music-tennis-Glacier Park summer also found me in St. Moritz, Switzerland (luxury hotels); Rimini, Italy (beaches for Europeans); Hilton Head, South Carolina (elitist enclave); Jackson Hole, Wyoming (high altitude skiing); and New York City (restaurants).

You commonly move from place to place and topic to topic. When you tell other people about your itineraries, they ask if they can carry your suitcase.

One of my colleagues is almost always on the go. His experiences are characteristic. "I just got back from the National Storytelling Festival in Jonesboro, Tennessee. I'll be home for only a week, then we'll be on the go with a student group in Europe, then to San Juan at the Caribe Hilton or Barbados, Sam Lord's Castle. . . ."

A former student writes from Finland: "Just heading into the Savo region. Chains of pine islands, shimmering lakes and steam barges, even a medieval castle. In Kotka, a Baltic isle linked by a bridge to the mainland, we biked to the country sauna; later, we ate *kalakukku*, which is fish baked in rye pastry crust."

You don't have to travel all the way to Scandinavia; diversity also awaits at nearby places. Explore Cape Cod from Boston; visit the Laurentian mountains from Montreal; drive to Santa Fe, New Mexico, from Pueblo, Colorado. The California wine country, Georgia's islands, the Wisconsin lakes are not too far from the cities. Everywhere, you'll meet and often interview interesting people, who bring a region to life. You are getting paid for learning something new and seeing new areas, or truly observing the familiar for the first time.

Once you become a travel writer, even an occasional one, the profession gets into your blood. Paul Theroux calls it "a whole way of life"; the excitement seldom wanes and you have to keep going. One English colleague puts it this way: "As soon as you come back, the desire to go away again is very strong."

While waiting for a more distant journey, one author rode the New York subway for three solid days and wound up with a major story about the underground, much of it critical, all of it fascinating. What a topic! The New York City subway, with its graffiti, its muggers and other dangers! But why not? The genuine travel journalist can get involved in the most unlikely material.

Why Be a Travel Writer?

Bear in mind that if you publish some stories, you may suddenly exert a bit of influence upon your subject. Your descriptions could start the wheels of business and this means a certain measure of influence for you, the writer.

Let's say that you fell in love with a little known spa some-where. A travel agent or tour operator reads your raves, investigates and begins to send groups there. Or you were visiting Molokai a few weeks ago, and when your report appears, a reader decides on a vacation in Molokai; what's more, he and his family experience the same vibes you did on the island. He writes you and thanks you for suggesting this island. Surely, his letter reinforces your motivation to seek out other destinations, to keep writing.

Early in my career, at the behest of the Swiss National Tourist Office, I flew to visit a tiny, then unknown ski resort in the Bernese Oberland Alps. The piece ran on the United States West Coast, in Kansas City, Boston and Toronto. To my surprise, two large ski clubs decided to try the new ski center; the clubs were followed by so many smaller American and Canadian groups that two new hotels had to be built. That's the power of the *Reise-Journalist.*

In short, you have the possibility of helping people. Indeed, your main function is to assist the general public, as does a travel agent, in making choices and in knowing where to go, how to travel, what type of cruise to take and so on.

In some cases, your readers may not be able to budge from their homes, yet get vicarious thrills out of *your* adven-tures. You have the chance to entertain and enlighten them, as well as yourself. That, too, is satisfying.

A Prerequisite: Enthusiasm for Travel

Call it "wanderlust"—the lust to wander, the urge to keep moving and seeing the new, always suspecting that life is more interesting away from home. The late James Ramsey Ullman, author of mountaineering travel books, often spoke of the "elsewhere" men and women. Ask yourself: do you often want to be elsewhere? Does travel really pull at you? Mark Twain expressed his feelings for a mountainous place with the words, "I felt a tugging, a deep abiding tugging."

Do you feel that tugging? If you do, you might be a travel writer.

It is a very important question to ask yourself. You cannot enjoy being on the road without genuine enthusiasm.

For some of us, travel is almost a physical necessity. It springs from a chronic curiosity and desire to uproot ourselves. This is what happens, of course: you are uprooting yourself when you are visiting Australia or Algeria or China. You are absorbing a new world and its people. Travel involves understanding a place, and this is what distinguishes you from the average tourist. The tourist may race through the landscape, seeing buildings and having a few beers in a Gasthaus in Heidelberg. But the professional travel writer actually explores in depth.

Mark Twain's "tugging" is a worldwide phenomenon. Kurt Tucholsky, a writer who lived during Nobel Prize winner Thomas Mann's times, was drawn south to Venice, to Florence, to Palermo. Tucholsky was vociferous about his needs: "I hear a locomotive's whistle in the night, far-away places shout their longing and I turn over in my bed and think 'Traveling!' "

Someone claimed that "suffering makes you deep, travel makes you broad; in case I get my pick I'd rather travel."

And Robert Louis Stevenson expressed his own eagerness by saying, "For my part, I travel not to go anywhere but to go. I travel for travel's sake."

To be sure, I recently returned from Molokai, and I think already of the cruise that will take me to Portugal and to Spain and to London. I immediately send letters of inquiry to Tourist Offices of certain nations in Europe trying to assist me with details.

When I come back there will be another trip and another. Then the ski season arrives, and a new gondola lift has to be checked out or a new important hotel has to be inspected.

You are constantly, magnetically pulled to the world's four corners. The great affair is to move.

You can be living your stories to the hilt, sharing them with your readers. Thus:

Every morning and all afternoon, the famous Spanish sun pierces the porthole of your cabin, a regular ritual. Your cruise vessel sails in a southwestern direction of 14 knots. The ship is a thing of beauty, immaculately white. Some passengers stretch out on chaises on deck, soaking up the warmth and breathing the sea air.

On Main Street, the merchants sell baskets of local cherries, strawberries, red currants, gooseberries, blueberries, raspberries. What a picturesque community! You sit in the chestnut tree gardens of the Bad Osterfingen country inn; you linger over tender veal in cream sauce and the region's wines.

Hello there, golf enthusiasts: This must be your paradise. Fairways in all directions, three nine-hole courses with appropriate names like "Tall Pines" and "Great Oaks" scattered across 800 green acres.

Lost Valley Ranch. Soothing Mountains Ranch. Singing River Ranch. Tumbling River. Lazy H. Peaceful Valley Dude Ranch. C Lazy U. Endearing names in idyllic remote locations. A western dude ranch vacation!

You sip your *mai tai* drink and chew macadamia nuts, listening to the melodies that melt the heart. After the day's sports, your body sings its own song, sings of Hawaii's action-filled Big Island.

That evening, step up onto one of the Mazatlán hotel balconies. The scent of the sea is in the air. The palms sway. The surf sounds compete with the marimba tones. The ambience is warm. The band sings meltingly, *"Capri, c'est fini."* It isn't, of course. It just seems that way, at Mazatlán.

Apart from experiencing your voyages—and rendering them true to life for your reader—there is a third dimension, your memory of past trips.

You will never forget the unusual sights of a glacier climb in Oregon, the sun-drenched colors of the silent Moroccan desert, the threatening bulkiness of elephant herds in the Kenyan bush. You still feel the wetness of the rain as you squished through the Scottish heather. You still see row upon row of unnamed mountains in Alaska's Inside Passage. And while digested long ago somehow, the eight-course dinner at a Brussels, Belgium, restaurant will stick, if not to your ribs, to your mind.

You are ahead of others in the writing field because you can depict something more vividly. This enhances the reporting pleasure and effectiveness.

The Width and Breadth of Travel Journalism

Travel journalism (unlike baseball or football writing) gives you an amazingly wide choice of topics, approaches and slants.

The great number of choices was well explained by a Canadian editor in a talk to Canadian journalists. He pointed out that the term travel can be stretched to cover a world of subjects, each with a group of journals eager for the information. Just as an example of how big the subject is, take one subdivision: transportation by water. "From there you can go into barges, canals, ice boating, sailing, marine telephones, customs, harbors, freighters, shipboard etiquette, famous travelers, marine mysteries." He concluded that the above "provides more subjects than you could cover in a lifetime."

You can explore areas about which no one has written before. I remember an article by a *New York Times* correspondent who hit the jackpot by writing about skiing and ski centers in China. (If you come up with something really unique, you will no doubt sell it.)

I've reported on hiking in Scotland, African safaris, Mexican summers. A book on mountains allowed me to visit the major chains of many continents, and get the feel for the shape, size and proportion of most mountains. I learned about the people who live there as well.

A paperback on overseas jobs for Americans took me to Israel, Egypt, Sweden, Canada and other countries. A Wyoming and Montana travel guide meant the inspection of practically every hotel, motel, resort, restaurant, cafe, museum and tourist event in these two states. *Colorado: Off the Beaten Path* required me to hike many of Winter Park's lovely trails in order to depict them. (The forests are much quieter and healthier in Colorado than those in Germany's *Schwarzwald*, where the trees are dying from acid rain.)

A California woman and her husband, living on a twenty-eight-foot cutter, make the most of their nautical life. They write about the ports-of-call for *Yachting* and *Boating*, two well-paying magazines. Even cruise-ship travel offers a cornucopia of possibilities. You could write about the entertainment, the lectures or the sports at sea. You could concentrate on the cooks and stewards. You could visit the galleys: What provisions do they carry? How many hams, pounds of butter, lox, fruit and eggs does a seven-day cruise require? Or what about a short article on the captain of a cruise line, telling how he sees his ship, his duties, the passengers, what his life is like on land. You could research marine history. You can also write about the ports of call. It is all up to you. You are the *giornalista di viaggi*, as the Italians say.

Travel and Special Interests

I remember a trip I took to Germany with twenty other writers. We went from Frankfurt to Rothenburg-ob-der-Tauber and other medieval cities. It was interesting to see, later on as we exchanged published stories, how each writer had emphasized what he or she was interested in. One col-

league, for instance, focused on Rothenburg's complete history from medieval times to the present. He ignored scenery, people, food. Not a word about the architecture—the
Fachwerk structure of the buildings is actually unique. He
didn't comment on the bright red geraniums in the flower
boxes and on the balconies. He didn't paint us pictures;
instead, he gave us a complete history of the town.

Another colleague took an altogether different approach: He made copious notes of the restaurant meals. He
described the meaty breakfasts, the *wurst* for lunch, the *eis-
bein* (fat pigs' knuckles) for dinner. He concentrated on the
kitchens of the *Gasthäuser*.

Still other people on the trip sallied forth beyond
Rothenburg into the pastoral countryside. One journalist
discovered that the farmers rented rooms for as little as
$10 per night, which made an intriguing farm story.

All of the above point to one important lesson: On *your*
travels, you can pursue *your* personal interests. In short, as
you reach a location, you can explore it for your own purposes. It may take a day or two to decide on a slant; in fact,
even the professional travel reporters often arrive at a destination without the faintest idea of what they'll find there.
Only later do they develop a theme and know what they
want to write about. Throughout the process, they maintain
a sense of discovery. Then, suddenly, personal interests
come into play and they're launched.

Recreation

Thanks to the North American public's greater leisure
time, any story with a recreation angle could be of interest
to readers. Some writers actually earn part of their liveli-
hood with ski writing, for instance. They spend their winter
on the slopes, looking for new or unusual resorts, new ski
lodges or skier's hotels, new trails, new diversions on the
snow. They may write about Nordic cross-country retreats.
What's new at the resorts? And how do the ski areas differ

from one another? For some more sedentary journalists, recreation in winter means snowmobiles; for others, old-fashioned sleigh rides. A member of the United States Ski Writers Association told a university writing class, "If you live in the mountains somewhere in North America, then winter sports are a ready-made subject, a natural." Travel features can deal with your personal recreational interests. Do you like the ocean? You can write about snorkeling, scuba diving, para sailing, surfing, trolling for marlin in Mexico, or beachcombing. To some, recreation means houseboating, canoeing, kayaking, white-water river rafting, horseback riding, backpacking, hiking, even ballooning. Jeep tours to western ghost towns appeal to some readers; trout fishing to others. Trekking from hut to hut in the Swiss Alps makes for good recreational pieces. Other outdoors-minded writers have combined bicycle touring with travel stories. For many years, I've written about tennis ranches, tennis clinics, tennis hotels, and resort tennis programs. I'm partial to global spas and their various programs, to "beauty farms" where you engage in sports to lose weight.

The Arts

Do you have a keen appreciation for art? How about a tour of the Santa Fe or Taos galleries? Would the art museums of New York, Washington, D.C., Los Angeles, Chicago, London, Indianapolis, Toronto be of personal interest? Could you weave an article around a summer art workshop in Oregon, Wisconsin or on Cape Cod? Would a week's trip to Avignon—and a tour of painters' studios—be the kind of feature you'd like to write? Could you return to Florence's *Uffizi* or *Palazzo Pitti* art galleries for a fresh look and a short newspaper report? Would the architecture of Venice lend itself to an article? Some writers have done a great job describing the paintings and statuary in the world's large cathedrals.

Writing in this field could mean arts and crafts fairs
too; thousands of these take place every summer from coast
to coast.

The field could include buying carpets in Turkey, hand-
made leather goods in Italy and wood carvings in Austria. I
once did a feature about the *souk* and its wares in Marrakech, Morocco.

Music

Some writers like popular or rock music; others are
enthralled by symphonies, operas, chamber orchestras, piano soloists. Certainly, music festivals can become a fitting
subject for travel stories. Luckily, these summer events are
numerous and accessible. You could be visiting the Marl-
borough Festival in Massachusetts, Tanglewood on the East
Coast, Spoleto in the south, Aspen in the Rockies. If this is
your year for Europe, think of Salzburg, Lucerne, Bayreuth,
Edinburgh. Naturally, there you must have an affinity for
Mozart, Beethoven, Schubert, Verdi and others. Writing
about music festivals doesn't mean that you have to review
the performances. You could leave this to the music critics
if you prefer. But take note of the performers who were
there (or will be there next season), details about the community where the event is held, and the quality of major
hotels. You need to answer the reader's questions: What is
the atmosphere like? Is it actually possible to get tickets, or
is every seat sold out for years in advance, as for the Wagner
Festival in Bayreuth? What will the weather be like? Your
readers must expect sudden rainstorms that thunder and
wet-slap their ears at Spoleto. The Charleston, South Carolina, humidity makes you wipe your brow all the time.

My own personal interests include serious music. I
once went on a memorable classical music cruise. The cast
made it easy to come up with a good story. Violinist Isaac
Stern was aboard, along with flautist Jean Pierre Rampal,
pianist Emanuel Ax and trumpeter Maurice André. There

were so many pianists that we could not hear them all. Opera star Jessye Norman was there, singing at sea and on land. It was an extraordinary thrill to hear all these great artists rehearse. As the vessel steamed through the Caribbean Sea, one could only immerse oneself in the music.

Some ships offer country western music cruises. Or you could travel to Nashville and write about the musical scene there.

It's *your* choice. Wherever you find music, there may be a story.

Adventure

Adventure travel is a big field indeed; it doesn't mean that you have to climb Mt. Everest or push toward the North Pole on snowshoes or describe your swim across the English Channel. "Adventure," also known in its tamer form by editors as "off-beat travel," simply means heading for places where the masses haven't been yet and where most of the modern conveniences may not exist.

The thirst for the off-beat may partially explain Paul Theroux's success. A writer for decades, Theroux has traveled by train to Chittagong in Bangladesh, to Peshawar in Pakistan. His train odysseys to Darjeeling, Calcutta and Leningrad are pure adventure and well described.

I myself once had a Theroux kind of experience. I spent three harrowing, wholly paranoid adventurous days and nights in Bucharest, Romania. It seemed unlike any city I'd ever been to. I was sure that my room at the hotel was wiretapped. I was certain that the furtive, unshaven man who wanted to buy postcards in the old Imperial Park was an *agent provocateur,* ready to hand me over to Romania's version of the KGB, to linger forever in prison. I was fascinated by the manner in which an American temporarily behind the Iron Curtain was viewed. Actually, the purpose for my trip was to report on the "Gerovital" Clinic, where you could supposedly be made young again by injections of novocaine into your arms. The escape by train from the gloomy Bucharest station, through a night of police searches of every compartment to the cheeriness of Vienna, was pure Theroux.

William Buckley has written fascinating *New Yorker* reports and books about his sailing voyages to the Marshall Islands, the Johnston Atoll, the island of Kosrae, complete with many other landfalls and the forty-knot winds and scary moments at sea.

Adventure travel could also take place close to home. One writer boarded a commercial yacht with other bird, mammal and reptile watchers; the ship set out to the Baja, California, waters, complete with lecturers and the passengers taking innumerable photos.

Restaurants and Hotels

As a travel journalist you can also elect to write about restaurants. Everyone eats and has opinions about a bistro, a café, a gourmet palace, or the local Italian, Greek, Mexican, or German eatery. (Most editors like "roundups," the discussion of *various* establishments although some magazines sometimes zero in on just one, usually famous, restaurant.)

In any case, you could exploit the taste bud experience; it is part of travel, too.

Likewise, many readers have stayed at a major hotel, perhaps to attend a convention.

What is the hotel's essence, its character?

Who are the guests?

What are the hostelry's attributes?

How were you treated?

Hotel stories are especially in demand when it comes to writing about a major city like New York, London or Los Angeles. Refurbishments go on all the time. Some new construction is of interest, too. "Manhattan's Newest Hotels" can be a useful article.

History and Archaeology

Some authors are not especially keen to report on the present. They prefer the past. Such travel scribes do historical features.

One such colleague has done superbly with articles about Quebec City, Saint John, New Brunswick and Halifax, Nova Scotia. She visited these places in order to describe practically every building and its history. The same can be done in Rothenburg-ob-der Tauber, Copenhagen, Colonial Williamsburg, Mystic Seaport, New Orleans and a hundred other places.

Likewise, an interested, educated writer can focus on the study of past cultures in Egypt, Greece, Arizona and a host of other archaeological sites.

Chacun à son gout. Everyone to his taste.

A Few Words about Money

Ah, to be a travel writer! The variety of possibilities! The joys of the journeys!

But how about *money?* Indeed, as one hard-boiled old-timer often tells beginners, "Where's the *check?*"

Travel journalism has brought wealth to only a few practitioners. Most of these men and women authored successful, royalty-producing books, a few of which actually became bestsellers. In the same vein, certain guidebook creators like Arthur Frommer, Eugene Fodor, and the late Temple Fielding all became extremely affluent from their books, which are now written and edited by others. To be sure, numerous longtime travel book specialists make a decent living from books. You will easily recognize names like Robert Kane, Robert Fisher, Norman Ford, Ian Keown; all earn a handsome living from their book craft.

Top earners also contribute to the major magazines such as *Travel & Leisure, Vogue, Condé Nast Traveler, Town &*

Country and *New York* magazine, which pay surprisingly large sums for 2,000-word articles. Last, a handful of travel journalists are associated with powerful syndicates which sell newspaper columns of these lucky few to hundreds of papers in North America. One typical example is the Times Mirror Syndicate. Other travel writers earn an excellent living as travel editors on the staff of major newspapers such as the *Los Angeles Times, Chicago Tribune, New York Times* and many more.

Certainly, money is made by freelancers who work for the book market, major and lesser known magazines, and hundreds of newspapers just from time to time. Many such travel writers hold full-time jobs in public relations, advertising, teaching, travel agencies or non-related professions. Yet they still gross $3,000 to $8,000 a year from part-time freelance writing. When you consider that most newspapers pay $10–$15 for a story, you can see how hard one must work.

The opportunities—large or small—do become clear if you study the tourism business.

Figures tell the story.

Internationally, tourism and travel are now a $750 billion industry influencing even the balance of trade, the environment and politics. Visitors provide foreign exchange earnings, especially to developing countries.

Of those billions, the cruise industry alone contributes $1.2 billion. (This is something to keep in mind as you're sitting down to write your cruise-ship story.)

Even in a bad terrorism year more than $5.5 billion are spent by Americans on overseas trips. And every year more passports are being issued. Airline expansions and profits, new routes, and mergers add to the picture.

Apart from the United States tourists' spending $40 million a year òn domestic and worldwide travel, there is of course another important figure for the writer. Indeed, how about the outlets for newspaper travel journalism? More than 150 newspapers contain weekend travel sections, some of which can be considered freelance travel markets, even though many newspapers rely on wire-service and staff-written stories. Every year, hundreds of new magazines, all with a travel piece or two, see the light of day. Newspapers add special travel pages, and bookstores clamor for new travel guides.

You don't have to be an established travel writer to earn money. Even as a novice you can pick your own destination, charge it to your credit card, or dig into your savings and go. Then offer your story when you get home.

What if you *don't* sell your initial output?

For many such writers, the travel itself is the reward.

2

Traits and Talents

What Makes a Good Travel Writer?

What common traits do the best travel writers share? What is required for the newcomer to the field? What kind of talent must you have? Precisely, who is suited to this kind of work?

First of all, you need the reporter's skills and discipline. It begins with the reporter's innate curiosity. Unless you're deeply interested in a subject, it will be difficult for you to get sufficiently involved to write well about it.

Observation

The true reporter has a keen sense of observation, which is made up of sensitivity and a subtle perception. His/her eyes are wide open. At the beach, even in a bathing suit, the note pad is poised for notes, or the mini-tape recorder is at the ready. His/her antennas are receptive and quivering from the first moment. What are the colors of the water, the sand, the bathers? What sounds can one hear?

And that straw basket of fresh oily doughnuts carried by the coffee-colored Mazatlán kid, what do the bakery goods smell like? How about the carpet/blanket vendors and their many-hued wares?

One can be mesmerized, yet still be objective and observant.

In time, you should get the complete feeling for a place. All along, you are a camera with a lot of film, shooting saturation-style, bringing together many pictures.

"A traveler without observation is like a bird without wings," goes one old proverb. Some writers are lucky enough to be naturally perceptive; others must develop the skill. Some fortunate ones travel to a far-flung summer school, where they can write and paint at the same time, one skill re-inforcing the other. As one observer has said, "A thousand Frenchmen may walk down a Paris street and, turning the corner, forget the place. A Toulouse-Lautrec walking down the same street would see with his shrewd eyes and remember with his artistic force of retention." Try to see like Toulouse-Lautrec or like Mary Cassatt or other painters whom you admire. This is a good habit to get into.

To be a *journaliste de voyage* allows you to be a Monet or a Manet or a Gauguin, picking up the sights as a painter would. You can reflect on paper the shape of a sea coast, a Tibetan village, the French Riviera's hillsides. I began as a water color painter while going to school in Florence for four years as a teenager. Art has a tremendous influence on my life as a writer. Once you see in color and in shapes, you are ahead of others because you can depict something more vividly.

Unless you observe well and note details, editors will wonder if you visited the place you're writing about. One travel magazine editor rejected a report with the brutal words, "This sounds as though you've never been to the French Riviera. Or did you *really* see Nice, Toulon, Villefranche or St. Paul de Vence?"

Observation is impossible without fascination and im-
mersion. A city should make you curious or furious; it
should reach out for you and grab you. Observation doesn't
allow for much leisure time. Whether you're visiting Washington, D.C., Molokai, Tangiers or the Galapagos Islands,
you should engage yourself fully in a story. You are *at work*.
When Kate Simon visited Rome to research a travel guide,
for instance, she returned to the Piazza Navona five times to
observe the colors and mood at dawn, noon, in the afternoon, evening and at night.

Great authors are always observant and their writings
can serve as models. Here's Mark Twain in Baden-Baden:

"Baden-Baden sits in the lap of the hills, and the
natural and artificial beauties of the surroundings are
combined effectively and charmingly. The level strip
of ground which stretches through and beyond the
town is laid out in handsome pleasure grounds, shaded
by noble trees and adorned at intervals with lofty
and sparkling fountain-jets. Thrice a day a fine band
makes music in the public promenade before the Con-
versation-House, and in the afternoons and evenings
that locality is populous with fashionably dressed people of both sexes.

A good many of these people are there for a real
purpose; they are racked with rheumatism, and they are
there to stew it out in the hot baths. These invalids
looked melancholy enough, limping about on their
canes and crutches, and apparently brooding over all
sorts of cheerless things. People say that Germany, with
her damp stone houses, is the home of rheumatism."

By contrast, a less perceptive writer than Mark Twain
might merely supply the bare bones about Baden-Baden,
which deprives the material of its authenticity and charm.
Thus: "Baden-Baden is situated among hills; the spa has lots
of trees, water fountains and public promenades. Many of
the guests here suffer from rheumatism."

One longtime editor sums up the subject: "Skip the obvious story and come up with something fresh and revealing, even if it seems oblique."

The "viewpoint," "slant" or "approach" to a subject often emerges only on location. Then you run with it.

Some years ago, the *Los Angeles Times* Sunday supplement sent me on a trip south with a singles group. I toured Mexico City and Acapulco with these singles for about ten days.

There were thirty-four women and four men.

Expecting to write about romance, I instead discovered that on this vacation, the ladies remained lonely. The women paid $1,500 in the hope of meeting a nice man. Instead, they met only other women.

What happened next? There were two Mexican guides along, as well as a burly bus driver. Very slowly many of the American women gravitated toward these Mexican men who had their own wives and families at home.

From a story angle, these developments proved more interesting than the expected romance among singles.

Naturally, a writer should never arrive with preconceived notions. A small measure of skepticism is useful, too. Let's say you read somewhere about a unique German clinic where they make you sit in a bathtub filled with mud. The mud is supposed to rejuvenate you. Could you possibly visit Baden-Baden and check out that treatment for a travel piece? If so, you may want to approach your story with wide open eyes, the clinic's propagandists notwithstanding. Skepticism and humor can contribute to interesting copy if used with discretion.

Accuracy

Accuracy is the key. Readers will take your advice at face value and rely upon it; indeed, a few travelers actually carry your clipped story with them to foreign lands.

It is not difficult to be accurate. You merely have to double check a fact. Example? You are told by a tour guide in Santa Fe, New Mexico, that a code forbids any building higher than three stories in the center of town. Such a statement can be verified by looking at the edifices on your own. You can also question the local shopkeepers or a Santa Fe librarian.

An Ontario editor puts it this way:

"God help the travel writer who has assumed something, taken a brochure at face value, or written something on somebody else's say so. He's going to get caught. Really caught because some of his readers are going to take pen in hand and write to his editor in order to correct the error."

The moral is obvious. Even if your errors get by the editor they often will not get by the readers. Newspapers receive letters by the dozen.

A writer once made the slight mistake of writing about a trip to Ixtapa, Mexico. She mentioned a certain air carrier. She mentioned how great the flight was. Actually the airline had given up the route just about three weeks before the article appeared and she didn't know about it. So the paper got a number of complaint letters. This created havoc with the paper's accuracy.

The best travel writers have honesty in common. They cannot be swayed by public relations people but use their own eyes and instincts. They are not naive. Professionals aim to be objective; they feel responsible to their readers.

Humor

Honesty can often be combined with a touch of humor, which makes your verdict more acceptable.

"Humor is a scarce commodity," admits one travel expert.

Naturally, what seems funny to one person may not amuse another. Humor is subjective; so it might be a good idea for the novice to try out the piece on a few friends first. Was your material truly entertaining? Did they *all* laugh?

Before entrusting your article to the (usually hard-boiled) editor, ask yourself: 1) Do I really know my subject? 2) Is it new? 3) Does it stick to the *truth* even if written in a humorous way? One writer may get the most humor out of some airlines' chronic loss of baggage. Another may mine the overselling of hotel rooms or a honeymooning couple's impossibly small cruise cabin with single beds.

Here's how one can depict the current ski scene, tongue-in-cheek:

"A lot of pampered types are being moved upward in motorized contraptions that go by the name of Ski-Doo, Snow-Cruiser, or Ski-Daddler. No muscle. In some resorts even the supposedly rugged Ski Patrol is mechanized to take broken-bone victims to the First Aid Station. A Ski-Doo ride for maybe 200 yards. And what happens at the hospital? In the Aspen, Colorado, clinic everybody with a broken leg receives a bunch of flowers." How'd you like that, for a soft life?

Skiers today smooch, drink wine, discuss exotic ski techniques or sex or fashion and finally crawl down the easy slopes at a snail's pace.

Gone are the days when a new ski area dared to call itself "Suicide Six," or "Satan's Ridge." Nowadays, ski complexes receive tame names like "Heavenly Valley" and "Sugar Bowl." And sweetness reigns when it comes to naming the ski runs. Now it's the "Maiden Lane," the "Yodler."

Or Bob Hope's house in Palm Springs:

"Who has the most extravagant setup? Count on billionaire Bob Hope who now owns six homes in Palm Springs. Some are for guests; Hope himself lives in the mountainous 'Southridge' section near Walter Matthau. Bob Hope's $12 million house is so large that local folks call it the 'Hope Airline Terminal.' The adobe actually has seventeen bathrooms, dining for 300 persons, 23,000 feet of living space, and even a large interior waterfall. You also learn that the comedian feeds filet mignon to his poodles.

"Your tour guide points to the flying saucer-shaped edifice from a mile below. Bob Hope doesn't want the buses to come close. If you drive your car up the steep Southridge

highway, you'll notice various reminders to stay out. On the
mountain top a plainsclothesman steps out of a control
post. He wears a large gun. On the gate, a sign reads 'Guard
dogs trained to attack!'"

Flexibility and Other Attributes

What other traits and talents should the travel journalist possess? Adaptability is one of the major ones. You must
adjust to extreme heat and to bitter cold; you need the physical stamina to handle long flights. You must be flexible
enough to accept airline delays, waiting at airports, substandard trains, unaccustomed meal times.

Certainly, the study of a country's history and customs
will be helpful before arrival on location, where the North
American yardstick often doesn't work. Foreign languages?
These are useful but nonessential; *patience* with other people's customs and attitudes seems far more important. Likewise, the open mind, genuine curiosity, tact, acceptance of
inconveniences are the essentials for the professional travel
person. Good health helps, too, around the world, all the
way from Algeria to Zambia.

In the end, you need to overcome adversity for the
most vital of all tasks—writing your manuscript.

Credibility and a Critical Eye

How do you gain credibility with editors and readers?

First of all, believability is established through authoritative reporting—that is not only true but also convincing.
This becomes especially easy in some foreign countries
when you can season your text with a few foreign words.
Listen to Kate Simon in Italy, for instance:

"Many of the lovely words that purl out of Italian
mouths, you will notice, deal with eating: 'Ha mangiato
bene?' 'Si mangia bene.' 'Che mangiamo oggi?' 'Dove mangiamo?' All are invitations to long, animated discussions."

The difficulty of getting even a small hotel room of low quality brought my Paris story to life. I titled it "Paris Today: with Candor":

"At the Tourist Office in the Gare du Nord, the line for rooms formed on the left and right. As usual, all the large hotels were sold out. 'Il n'y a rien!' snapped the lady behind the counter. 'No space!' It took her more than an hour to locate a bed at the tiny 'Du Brabant' on the Rue des Petit Hotels. The bathroom had neither door nor towels; the breakfast of hard French bread came without plates or napkins."

I had obviously been there.

Many beginners in the field, and even some old-timers, confuse travel journalism with public relations. You are not writing a PR release.

Newspapers see travel writers as journalists who provide a true picture with the plusses and a few minuses, the positives and also a negative point or two. Some mini-criticism makes for veracity and increases the realism of your report.

Superior editors expect you to be opinionated, to take a stand, to have strong views about a place. Some beginners have failed because their copy is all sweetness; the material is aimed to please a resort or the city fathers, for instance. An East Coast editor agrees. He tells prospective contributors: "We strive to report and to tell it like it is. And freelancers who send puffery get it right back unless they have a track record of telling it like it is because we feel very strongly about the responsibility to the reader."

Another publishing executive explains it this way: "It is completely possible to be blunt, to include negatives without being blackballed by a carrier or destination. It's all in the reasonableness of the tone. This takes increasing understanding from writers. These are consumer-oriented times and without bluntness and without that understanding, travel writing will decline. In San Diego we found that honest, friendly, reasonably stated negatives, not petty bitches, are accepted gracefully by the newspapers."

A longtime *Washington Post* travel editor stresses that he welcomes submissions but he then goes on to say:

"We do not believe that travel stories should be designed specifically to please either the carriers or the destinations concerned. Unfortunately all beaches are not always clean, the sun does not always shine, all hotels do not always offer fine food and unblemished service, and bargains are not always bargains. Since all tourist areas are not the same they cannot be treated the same. A story can be both critical and honest without being unfair or unbalanced."

The editor further emphasizes that the newspaper's "primary responsibility is to our readers," that the newspaper is beholden to the readers and it is up to you to give a fair picture for other readers who want to go to your rain forest or the music festival. The public wants to know the absolute truth. This is vital if you are to fulfill the role as a travel reporter, as the journalist.

The mature, sophisticated traveler, the inexperienced novice—and all stages in between—want to know what a place is like. Readers have the right to all the facts before they spend their money.

A travel editor agrees, "Too many freelancers shy away from criticism and are like a camera with a rose-covered lens." Don't write like a PR agency, or like a brochure. You're expected to tell it like it is.

These rules apply especially to quality newspapers, all of which are independent of their advertising departments and can generally run anything they please. They may not want to accept a totally negative story, however. Likewise, some travel guides prefer that contributors forgo the critical. Their rule: If a hotel or restaurant is substandard, the writer simply leaves it out. It is wise to ask the editor what the policy is on his publication.

The old *Holiday* Magazine, which was publishing Faulkner, Steinbeck, Michener and other big names during the fifties, was famous for its high standards of frank reporting. Unless a writer really captured a place, he was *persona non grata.*

My files contain superb examples of professionals stating their complaints in articles. A *New York Times* correspondent describes the horrendous language problems in Peking hotels. Taki, the witty European aristocrat and traveler, warns against the "hawk-eyed Spanish jewelry dealers looking for victims in Marbella. If they don't get you, sharp-tongued real estate promoters will. Stay away!" A San Jose travel editor gently scolds London's famous Claridge Hotel for his being forced to sit more than four hours in the lobby until his room was made up. "We had been up almost thirty hours and needed a bed and bath soonest. We looked like last week's oatmeal. . . ."

3

Travel Writing Techniques

How to Choose a Locale

Contrary to what you might think, a free-lancer is never told what to write about by a newspaper travel section editor or a magazine editor. The choice of a locale is entirely up to the journalist. So is the approach. The situation is different for travel writers employed by major newspapers who head occasionally for a location with editorial instructions; likewise, contributing editors and staff writers for magazines leave with definite assignments. So do a few rare "name" magazine contributors.

What does all this mean to the freelance travel journalist?

Let's say you'd like to do a Colorado ski story. Should you write about mega-resorts like Aspen or Vail? Not necessarily. Too many writers may have already dealt with these resorts. The editors and readers are probably tired of these destinations. By contrast, you could focus on a tiny or lesser-known Colorado ski area. It may not be a household name with readers but it may be cheaper or offer some new activity. You might even find a ski hill which caters to beginners and rents out tiny little, skate-like skis.

To be sure, there has to be a magnetic pull: you can only write about a place that has always fascinated you. (Let us hope that it's one which you can afford.)

Whether it's a resort, an amusement park or a zoo, it should be non-hackneyed, perhaps even a little unconventional. (Avoid the old Disneylands; everyone has already been there.) If you pick a more ordinary locale, you must find some unique features. Kansas City? Write about the Crown Center with its enormous hotels, its theatres and fourteen restaurants in one compact area.

Neophyte writers often plan too broad a story about a locale. They will do all of Wisconsin in 600 words. Or all of Manhattan—including Chinatown, Wall Street, Third Avenue and Times Square—in 700 words. It is much better to zero in on one small facet of a town, a state or province. It could be a single street or unique museum. It could be a resort or a new shopping mall, complete with all the gossip, complete with architects who are being sued by a bus company.

Another editor, in a talk to a professional group, put it very succinctly, "I would rather read an article about cutting peats in the Irish bogs than a wholesale, generalized sweetmeat travel article. If I ever get to Ireland it will be because I want to smell the peat fires and squelch through a bar, not because the hills are emerald, the sky amethystine blue. Are the Irish very poor? Tell me because I have absolutely no objection to people being in financial straits as long as they are interesting, photogenic and talkative."

Steve Cohen picked a good, narrow focus by describing his honeymoon cruise on a much-touted ship which actually had the tiniest, most uncomfortable cabins afloat and the food was less than impressive. On another occasion, Cohen wrote about a western glacier that attracted summer skiers. In 600 words, he told us how they dress, how they picnic and cavort and tumble and enjoy themselves. The tableau was perfect. The glacier made for a compact story. Had he attempted to deal with the major northwestern glaciers, he might have failed. As a result of his choice, Steve Cohen managed to sell both stories to several newspapers.

Actually, a writer need not go far afield. For a starter, there is little point to jetlag all the way to the Tunisia Club Med or to Tahiti for an interesting story. You can get one in the nearest old mining town. You can pick a farming community with a decent roadside café and two antique stores.

One of my most successful stories took me to Cheyenne, Wyoming, and the "Frontier Days." What is a western rodeo really like? The cowboys, the bars, the dust, the animals, the smells all add up to a believable piece of writing.

If you live in New York City, you *don't* have to travel to the tip of Long Island. You could do Jones Beach, or a new museum in Brooklyn, or revisit Coney Island now. What's happened to that beach and amusement park? It would be interesting to read a story about the place you knew decades ago. Go back and describe the changes.

Note Taking

Some beginners are afraid of note taking because it is work; they just wander around a place, enjoying themselves. Actually, you can't procrastinate, and eventually, the task of gathering information in writing becomes a habit. (This is done via old-fashioned notebooks; a few writers carry tape recorders.)

The experienced critic—or travel journalist—looks, perceives, analyzes but always remains slightly distant, a bit reserved toward the subject.

Your first notes can be brief, as though they are unrelated images in your diary. On an outing to Waikiki, Hawaii, your notes might look like this:

Today I saw on Waikiki Beach:

- A man surfing with his black dog. The animal wore a wreath of flowers around his neck. A lei.
- A woman who had brought an enormous, many-hued parrot to the beach. She talked to the bird as I came by.
- A fencing school. All fencers wore white.
- A group of acrobats and would-be acrobats who used their children for shoulder and head stands, under a tall palm tree.
- A very old, very thin lady feeding bread to white pigeons, intermittently feeding herself. She sat contently under a Waikiki palm tree.

Now all of this material may not find its way into a story that you write about Waikiki. But some of it will be used. The point is that you can't tell ahead of time what you will need for your article.

As you begin to explore an area in some depth, you may wind up with scenic views, botanical data, fauna and flora. While being shown the island of Molokai by a photographer, I jotted down these emerging facts:

- red Hawaiian tulip trees
- ground is iron oxide red
- pineapple fields
- wild boar and deer in the hills
- bougainvillea, yellow plumaria
- herb harvests (small farms)
- white egrets
- coconut forests
- groves of macadamia nuts
- bamboos, ironwood trees, pili grasses, ferns
- basil and oregano grown here
- minimalist landscape reminding of Africa (Kenya?)
- wooded mountains
- mangoes, bananas
- green rolling hills
- watermelons, green beans, sweet potatoes, onions, alfalfa sprouts

- mynah birds in the trees
- native orchids
- kukui groves, kiawe trees
- hunters: quail, partridge

Thanks to the presence of a local Molokai photographer, you learn the names of the trees and other plants. You notice that the ground consists of red earth and you ask why. You're told that it's the iron oxide which gives it the red color.

That's research. It merely requires some questions and the ability to listen to the answers and write them down.

Research

Research? Editors don't do it for you. Nor do they supply any materials. In addition to what the local people tell you, some digging should already be done at home a few days before you venture into what may be an exotic territory for you. You should be hungry for some prior library information. (Your librarian will have some recent travel guides.) Likewise you can study some travel agency material as well, and perhaps pick up a book at your favorite book store. Find out about the history, geography, politics, climate, customs, food, dress of the place. (It is a good idea to bring your notes to your story location.)

In Switzerland, the nearest *Kurdirektor* (tourist official) will bury you in material; in North America, practically every state, province and city employs a PR person who can supply publicity releases. This will help you to achieve some depth on location. You won't be accused of superficiality, or of whipping up a story (as some misguided writers do) from the top of your head after just a few hours visiting. A Spanish sage said it best, "He who bring home the wealth of the West Indies must carry the West Indies with him." In short, you need to assemble a certain intellectual baggage for a trip. Reading certainly helps.

Some beginners make too few notes while researching; they do not go deeply enough. Indeed, it's okay to over-research for your first stories, to come up with too much material. Eventually, you may reach a point where you bump into the same fact three times; then it's time to think of organizing some of your treasure house of information.

Some of your research may come from interviews while on location and could consist of quotes. These can be used very effectively in travel writing, to convey credibility and to make your story read well.

Organizing Material

On your last day "on location," it is a good idea to organize your notes; after all, you were just there and the impressions are still fresh. How do many professionals handle the sorting chores?

Take a pair of scissors and separate your various scribblings by subject, and then sort your scribbles into useful little piles. If you are doing a nuts and bolts type of story, for instance, you will have data about hotels, restaurants, local events and so on.

It isn't difficult to decide which paper mountain goes up front in your piece; the sequence of the rest depends on the story itself and its emphasis. While you work, a title will slowly emerge, and the well-organized paper piles will make the writing comparatively easy.

Some authors prefer to do their organizing and writing chores after the trip, *at home.* This procedure doesn't always work out for the novice who might be tempted to forget all about the story. And your writing may be most effective while the scene is still alive in your mind.

Actually, you are best off to spend a few solo hours in your hotel room. Privacy is essential, of course. If you travel with a spouse or friend, that beloved person will have to stay away while you concentrate on your story.

4

How to Write with Style

Style and the Travel Story

"Language! Man's greatest invention!" wrote Franz Kafka. "The style should be the author's, *if* he's an author and if he has style," Wolcott Gibbs told us.

The new travel journalist need not worry unnecessarily. Good writing comes with experience. In due time, your descriptions will be graphic and vivid. You will learn to avoid dullness.

Meanwhile, here are some style pointers:

Keep it Short and Simple

Luther said it best: "The fewer words, the better prayer." Instead of saying, "Each and every one of us" consider "All of us." Likewise, the brief word "now" is better than "At the present time."

You need only recall the architect's dictum, "Less is more." Prune your adjectives. Go easy on adverbs. Remember that your story competes for the reader's time, along with television and books.

In the last century, it was still permissible to ramble. Now, you are expected to write tightly. Paper and newsprint are more expensive and printer's wages have gone up.

Make every word count. Robert Turnbull, a Canadian travel journalist, shows you how: "The cabin was dark except for some dim blue lights in the ceiling. Passengers slept; now and then a match flared and a cigarette end glowed. Once a white-coated steward flitted like a ghost down the aisle; and even the thrum of the jet engines, never loud at any time, seemed muted during those dark hours.

"The mood was one of infinite loneliness, of being suspended, unmoving in space. A small taste, perhaps, of how astronauts must feel."

And see how simply composer Verdi states his case:

"I adore art . . . when I am alone with my notes, my heart pounds and the tears stream from my eyes, and my emotion and my joys are too much to bear."

Notice the easy rhythm of good prose; the sentences vary in length. (Pointer: Don't lengthen your sentences so much that your reader can't follow you any longer.)

Rhythm

An otherwise competent PR person sent out the following release for a music festival:

Although the 75-year-old Mr. Menotti, Spoleto's founder, is an old hand at the festival business having produced 29 in Italy, 10 in the United States and one in Australia, Mr. Argiris and Mr. Redden, both 36 years old, will be planning and executing this year's Spoleto Festival for the first time.

The sentence is obviously too long. The lines lack rhythm. Now listen to English author Sybille Bedford:

> "Winter in Venice. Arrival. The moment of doubt: will it be there, will it have subsisted—this grandest, this strangest, most fabulous of white elephants of the past? Can that magic still work on the inhabitant of an increasingly different world? The handing into the *motoscafo*, the bestowal of luggage—*signori!*—moments of Italian action."

Make Your Style Interesting

As you noticed, the British stylist varied her structure, and her meter. Her sentences surprise and delight us. One editor says: "Mix 'em up. Shrink 'em down. Stretch 'em out. Make 'em gallop. Make 'em funny. Make 'em sad. Make 'em abrupt. Make 'em languid."

Some journalists have an ear for language. William Zinsser, author of *On Writing Well*, points out that "the good writer of prose must be part poet." And it is true that some of the more literary American magazines often opt for poets to do their travel articles.

Never employ the same word on a page three or four times. (The only exceptions: "and" or "but.") In the (now defunct) "Empire" section of the *Denver Post*, a writer's excellent idea—a look at the sheepherders of Minturn, Colorado—was marred by using "sheep" *nine times* in a few hundred words. Yes, the occasional "lamb," "ewe" or "animal" would have been helpful.

Another example comes from the publications of a small performing arts center: "Mention *theatre* in London and one immediately thinks of the West End which houses many of the venerable and historic *theatres* that make up a large part of *theatre* (and even literary) history. Or, we think of the Royal Shakespeare Company performing at the Aldwych, and more recently, the National *Theatre* where one can see Paul Scofield, John Gielgud."

This is sheer laziness. The reviewer never bothered looking into her thesaurus. Result? Extreme monotony.

Even well-known newspapers have been guilty of repetition. "London Town can grate. And *when* it does, and *when* the old Samuel Johnson line, '*When* a man is tired of London, he is tired of life,' no longer sustains me." An awkward sentence. And worse: *three* when's.

When I did a pictorial book about the mountains of the world, I made sure that I used not just the words mountains, peaks, hills or crests. I also wrote of citadels, crenelations, uplifted blocks. Mountains? You can speak of cathedrals, buttresses, tiers, pillars, ramparts, faults. Of a massif, of mounds, eminences, galaxies.

Use Plain Language

Hopelessly old-fashioned, ponderous expressions that have long since bitten the linguistic dust are to be avoided. You can't get away with phrases like "Inasmuch as," "Attached hereto is my ms" or "Notwithstanding the fact that." Use "face" instead of "visage" and "stay" instead of "reside." (The opposite—the New Age language—has its own perils; some youth slang may be passé next week.)

Rohn Engh, a respected newsletter publisher, explains it well:

"Instead of attacking that blank sheet of paper in your typewriter as a technically perfect erudite report, consider it as a letter to a friend. Keep the tone and mood friendly. You can even go so far as to type in a fictitious "Dear Bill" at the top of your "letter." Never attempt to be "cute" in your writing. If something strikes you as extremely clever, then strike it out!"

I once read in a Canadian newspaper a description of an Austrian winter hiking center: "If you love snow but are a *f-fr-fraidy* cat on those scary ski slopes, here's a tiny hideaway tip, a plateau high in a remote corner of Austria where

other people go skiing (bless 'em) but my breed goes snow-
hiking." (The f-fr-fraidy cat is especially corny.)

Your descriptions should flow naturally. Nigel Buxton,
longtime *London Sunday Telegraph* travel columnist, is worth
studying:

"Dawn broke upon autumn mists over the river. The
sun rose and cleared the mists and illuminated the autumn
colours among the trees. There were roses and dahlias and
crysanthemums in the well-kept gardens of the hotel and an
admirable breakfast was punctually served."

Some authors have trouble controlling their preten-
tiousness. An article in a slick society magazine started this
way: "As every perspicacious peregrinator knows by now
..."—I never finished the piece.

Unfamiliar or inappropriate words only confuse the
reader. Don't show off; modesty is better. Remember George
Orwell: "Good writing is like a pane of glass." The author is
not trying to impress anyone.

No Clichés, Please

A first-class editor considers clichés fourth-class. One
example might be to over-use the word "fun." It is a cliché
in the eyes of sophisticated writers. You can do better. A
travel editor told a group of writers in Utah:

"If a friend informs you about witnessing a 'purple
sunset' over 'breathtaking majestic' mountains with 'quaint,
picturesque' villages, then you'd better find another friend."

One good rule? If you think that you're facing a cliché,
you probably are. Say it differently. Be creative. Close your
eyes before you commit a sentence to paper. (After listening
to a student's read-aloud prose, a famous author said darkly,
"My friend, this time you were not writing—you were
typing!")

Not long ago, a number of travel editors were asked
which words should be avoided. The experts came up with
the following clichés: Quaint, breathtaking, picturesque,

unique, spectacular, romantic, charming, towering cliffs, colorful costumes, the most beautiful city in the world.

What's wrong with the above words? They are simply too trite.

Always remember the dictionary definition: "*Cliché* describes any expression that was once fresh but has become stereotyped through frequent repetition."

Grammar, Punctuation and Spelling

Beware of slipshod writing! Always be 100% certain of a word. Check it out three times if necessary. Look into the dictionary for your spelling. One minor misspelled Mexican town would make you suspect in the eyes of the editor. He or she will not continue to read the article, having begun to distrust you.

A Denver writing student told me that he met with great resistance in trying to sell his combination of photos, photo captions and stories. It turned out that all his commas were in the wrong places.

Some writers avoid question marks. Should you? On the contrary: question marks wake up and stimulate the reader, making him think. To wit: May Sarton, a great stylist: "New England grips the heart. Is it partly because for all the beauty, life has never been easy here?"

A Caribbean roundup starts:

"What's the current situation at the Caribbean ports-of-call? Which islands are "in"? Where will the traveler encounter problems? What's new and where?"

Question marks enliven your text; at the same time just be sure not to over-use them.

How about exclamation points? The competent *journaliste de voyages* avoids them, if possible. A Texas editor once returned a novice's story because it wasn't, he explained "exciting enough." A week later, the Texan opened a manuscript envelope to find that same story, this time peppered with exclamation points.

Bad grammar can kill the clarity of your text. The editor tolerates incorrect syntax once or twice per page. After that, the entire manuscript, facts and all, can become suspect because it is evident that the writer is ignorant, or careless, or lazy.

More suggestions? Get hold of some paperbacks on the subject of good English. Read *The Elements of Style* by Strunk & White (Macmillan) or *Writing with Style: Conversations on the Art of Writing* by J. R. Trimble (Prentice-Hall). There are many more useful and interesting books on the English language.

Freshness and Vivaciousness

Good prose has *color*. It appeals to the senses. A sentence comes alive. Examples?

"The very name London has tonnage in it." (V. S. Pritchett)

"Illinois did a fair autumn day for us, crisp and clean." (Steinbeck)

"As the summer passes, the odors of the Cape become more intense, the string of salt marsh, the gamy smell of tomato vines, the mingled aromas of ripe grapes, cut grass, skunks and pines." (Theroux)

"There was music everywhere—choruses, string bands, brass bands, flutes, everything. I was so surrounded, walled in, with music, magnificence, and loveliness that I became inspired with the spirit of the scene and sang one tune myself." (Twain)

Freshness can be achieved with accurately spelled foreign words. How many? No more than one or two per page. *Cher ami, aficionado, gemütlich, Kitsch, cerveza, schlepp, Angst* are just a few examples. The late Joseph Wechsberg, who contributed some superlative travel articles to the *New Yorker*, would say, "foreign words should be used like pepper. Sparingly."

Adapting Your Style to a Publication

Would you like to get more editorial acceptances than some of your competition?

Here's a secret weapon: Study some sample stories in the newspaper travel sections you want to sell. Or if you aim for magazines, then analyze several articles.

Do so with great care.

The periodical press and the Sunday papers often have an "internal" style. Assess it. Try to follow it.

Specifics?

Begin your analysis with paragraphing. A paragraph can be as short as a single line.

Or it can ramble down an entire page.

If you study the rare travel exposé in the *National Enquirer*, for instance, you will notice a fresh paragraph for almost every sentence; conversely, *Harpers* or *The Atlantic Monthly* travel reports go on for half a page without a break. (Reason? The *Enquirer* has less experienced readers who need to pause frequently.)

The *average* newspaper doesn't want any literary fireworks. Orwell's "pane of glass" is better. The blocks of text consist of two to five lines. The language is simple.

A much-published colleague of mine, Illinois-based Randy Mink, shows you what I mean. Mink took his then 7-month-old baby Amanda on a Caribbean cruise.

Study his clear, unaffected writing:

> "Amanda enjoyed splashing in the pool and taking stroller rides on open decks. The stroller was a nuisance, however, when we had to pick it up for the stairs and raised doorways.
>
> At least once a day Mom and Dad would go to one of the lounges for a cola and peanuts, or for cookies at afternoon tea. One bar became our hangout because the Italian waiters, far away from their own families, doted over our dark-eyed, dark-haired girl and carried her around."

Mink entitled his story "Cruising the Caribbean with Infants & Children." He sold it to some thirty newspapers in the United States.

By contrast, consider the language used in the *Vogue* magazine travel sections. There is still a naturalness and vividness in the *Vogue* pages. But its sophisticated readers can be served up more complicated words. Bali is "a giddying series of unfamiliar fragrances. . . ." Egypt is "Cleopatra, of the alabaster brow, Pharoahs and Mamelukes. . . ."

Some magazines—*Town & Country, Gourmet, Esquire,* for instance—exude elegance from their travel stories, while others make simplicity their rule.

It is up to you to tell which is which.

5

Advantages and Obligations of Complimentary Travel

The Wonderful World of Complimentary Travel

These lines are written aboard a major five-star cruise ship, presently sailing from the Cayman Islands to Aruba. The ancient ocean shimmers outside; my cabin actually has large picture windows instead of portholes. The double bed, the settees, the extensive lights and mirrors, the stateroom video and a refrigerator are elegant—more like a movie set than an ordinary ship's cabin.

The cabin costs $6,000 for two weeks. This includes four fabulous meals a day, lots of entertainment and 4,000 Caribbean sea miles of transportation.

Yet I don't have to pay.

The voyage is complimentary.

A professional travel writer can enjoy the hedonistic delights of a ski resort (complete with airline ticket, condo and free ski lifts). The experienced pro stays at the best hotels, elegant and pricey country inns, tennis ranches,

43

"beauty farms," health spas and dude ranches in the wilderness. An invitation may be extended to visit New Zealand, Australia, Kenya or Austria. In many places, local tourist guides, car rentals and first-rate restaurant meals are made available.

Welcome to the wonderful world of subsidized travel! Unusual? Not for the initiated, the insider. Indeed, the professional travel writer receives many more offers than he (or she) can accept.

Here is the San Antonio Convention & Visitors Bureau's kind invitation, "Texas is celebrating its 150th birthday. We'd like for you to come to San Antonio to celebrate. Scheduled for March 6–9. Breakfasts, hosted lunches, dinner at good restaurants included. We'll gladly furnish the airline transportation. Please call me by 5 P.M. this Friday, February 28, if you can attend."

Or how about the siren call of glamorous Palm Springs, California—a wealthy place, wonderfully warm in winter. Thousands of swimming pools. Celebrities everywhere. The letter mentions a reception, a cocktail party, a brunch, a free Gray Line tour, cookouts, an aerial tram ride. For three days, most of the food is included.

The State of Nebraska periodically sends out letters like this one:

> Dear _____:
> We have a press tour of Nebraska you won't want to miss. It will include outdoor activities, touring historical sites and museums, canoeing, hiking in Nebraska's own national forest and visiting pristine wildlife refuges. This tour will feature the grasslands known as the Sandhills. The Sandhills are unique to Nebraska and the United States, with the only comparable areas being the pampas of Argentina or the steppes of Russia. This area offers western hospitality, wide-open spaces, and much bird and animal life.
> Please review our itinerary and contact us if you are interested in being a part of this press tour. We will

assist in making plane reservations and while in the state you will be hosted by the Division of Travel and Tourism and the communities and attractions you will be visiting.

A Florida inn chimes in with this friendly invitation:

Dear Mr. _____:
> Greetings from sunny Florida!
> You are invited to visit our resort, as my guest, and discover Vero Beach.
> I realize that the schedule of a travel journalist is a hectic one, which is the reason for this open-ended invitation . . . .
> Please, when your time permits for a retreat to our charming and unique community, phone me personally in advance and I'll make all the preparations.
> Looking forward to meeting you in the near future.
> Best regards,
> Director of Hotel Sales

All this is the destitute's dream: I'm sure that Mary McCarthy didn't accept any favors when she wrote so eloquently about Venice and Florence. I doubt that Paul Theroux asked for a gratis railroad ticket while researching *The Old Patagonian Express*. No, the "freebie" is for the colleague of modest means—someone who doesn't get five- or six-figure advances for books like the just-mentioned authors. Publishers of guides vary in their policies on payment for a writer's time and expenses. The freebies are extremely useful for the person of modest means. Most freelancers are poor, since travel writing doesn't pay that well. Any help is therefore appreciated; in fact, some pros welcome as many invitations as possible.

A colleague wrote to me: "Dear Curtis, We made it! Left Miami May 18 and I have not had to pay for one night's accommodations!" He drove all the way to Durango with his wife and his child. Every night, he would stay in a gratis hotel room. How could he do this?

Another colleague reports from a Chicago suburb: "This week, there have been offers ranging from a weekend in Oshkosh, Wisconsin, to Bermuda cruises, on two different lines. I was stunned by a call from Qantas [Australian airline], inviting all three of us [wife and child] to Australia. They're promoting family travel."

Unusual? Not at all. Legitimate? Yes.

Why should the travel industry be so gracious?

The answer is simple. Publicity. The mention of an air carrier, country, province, or resort hotel in a recognized travel journalist's article is better than—or as good as—a paid ad. Such a mention, or description, offers credibility. It influences the travelling public. An entire story about a cruise vessel, a fine hotel or airline meals is even more effective.

How the Pros Do It

To the novice writer, the gratis flight to Sicily or South America or Mexico seems a mystery. So is the invitation by a national tourist board.

Indeed, how does the professional go on a junket? What is the secret of complimentary travel?

The basic premise is simple.

You must persuade the prospective donor that you can do something for that airline or country or cruise line. You must convince your benefactor that you can render a valuable publicity service in exchange for the free ride.

You are expected to mention or, better still, describe a first-class hotel in a travel guide, or a magazine article or a newspaper piece for several papers.

Naturally, you can only be convincing if you have "credits," i.e., published samples.

You need to show proof of professionalism. You do this by means of *tearsheets*. These printed samples under your byline show that you are legitimate; you have supported other cruise ships (or airlines, railroads, resorts) with published material.

The tearsheet is the "open sesame" to most complimentary travel. It is the gold which gets you around the world.

Without this proof, you have no rights; you won't be taken seriously by an airline, hotel, resort or any other possible sponsor.

Once you can present enough evidence that you mention a sponsor, you can ask for invitations. You will find open doors, if you somehow can prove you are a travel writer.

When I say writer, it has to be *travel*. Someone asked me the other day whether she could parlay an article about nursing into a trip. No, an article about nursing is useless. You can't do anything with a hardware convention article. It has to be a travel story. And if at all feasible, that piece should mention an airline if you want an airline's support. Thus if you approach Pan Am or KLM, there should already be a mention of Lufthansa in one of your published articles. This shows that you've kept your promise. The travel donors' expectations are 1) that you actually write something; 2) that you place something; 3) that you basically do them some good, resulting in more business.

The key to free travel is the public relations manager, in some cases the public affairs person. If the company doesn't have one, then the sales manager or general manager may be useful.

Approaching the Powers-that-Be

It is not difficult to find out the name of the individual who is responsible for press contacts. Most large travel-related companies actually have 800 numbers. Thus, if you want to do a story in the Hawaiian Islands, you simply call your favorite airline which will provide the magic name of the PR person and the 800 number.

If you are an *established* travel journalist, you can make your first contact by phone. Does United Airlines organize any junkets to Hawaii next month? Or could you send in a proposal for a solo trip? You will no doubt be told to put it all in writing.

New travel journalists with some credits are best off to make their requests known in a letter.

What type of sponsor would be your best bet?

Keep in mind that airlines like to plug their new routes. That's where you might have the best chance. Conversely, new, or rebuilt, totally renovated hotels are a possibility.

The tourist offices of developing nations or tourist-minded countries are often eager to cooperate with professional travel specialists. Many of these junkets or individual trips are mentioned in the *Travel Writers Market Letter*, published by Bob Milne and listed in the bibliography. Almost every issue mentions the Canadian provinces or American states that have expressed their eagerness to host writers.

Request letters must be written on business stationery, with a printed letterhead, giving your address and indicating that you are a travel writer.

Your message can be brief. It can mention the prospective donors' public relations releases; more likely than not, you will have received such PR material.

Thus:

> Dear _____:
>
> Thanks for your faithful PR releases and letters.
>
> They whet my appetite. And of course, for the professional travel writer, the proof of the PR pudding is in the seeing.
>
> I write for many newspapers. Ask your airline contacts to fly me to the Maryland shore and host me for a few days while there.

I'm free during early August. I plan many weeks ahead. Hope you accept my challenge.
Cordially,

PS: A small dossier of published sample stories is enclosed; my specialties: beaches, excursions, tennis, restaurants.

Naturally, you will be judged by your tearsheets; the better the newspaper or the magazine, the more chances to travel.

If your letter doesn't spell out details, your PR contact may request more information. Here's an example from an airline corporate communications manager sent to one of my travel writing students:

J.Z., our executive vice president-marketing and planning, forwarded your brief note to our department for our evaluation and response.

I would like to ask you to provide much more comprehensive information on exactly who you write for, what areas you cover, what you would like from us and what you can do for us. If you follow through, we will be happy to respond to you.

Sincerely,
Manager, Corporate Communications

It is important to be as specific as you can. For instance:.

Dear _____:

This comes from a prolific travel writer who works for some 40 United States, Canadian and European newspapers.

You were kind enough to send me several PR releases.

I have never sailed with the Line. Would it be possible to come aboard for your September 8 or September 15 Canada voyages?

I can guarantee you much exposure. I always like unique itineraries as you'll see from the attached sample stories.

Thanks for returning the materials at your convenience. I work many months in advance and would appreciate a letter soon.

With best wishes,

Dates are important. A ski resort example:

Dear V.

It was nice seeing you at the various Ski Media functions. Your clipping service no doubt picks up my numerous mentions of your resort.

I plan to do a major roundup of COLORADO'S GONDOLAS

for the coming season. Because you've completely replaced your gondola, I'd like to take a special trip to your mountain to experience the new conveyance.

I'll be departing from Denver on February 26th, arriving at your area in the afternoon of March 2.

Could you book me into the Sheraton for March 2 and 3? (Checkout 4th.) The hotel would be mentioned, of course.

Anticipated thanks for getting back to me soon to confirm.

With best wishes.

The Writer's Obligations

What are the writer's obligations? First of all, pay attention to what your hosts have to say. For instance: you have been invited to Ft. Lauderdale, as a guest of the local chamber of commerce. They have arranged for a chamber of commerce chief to have dinner with you. Your host will probably bring a press kit with information about the city. Study the material; it could be helpful for your story. And listen to your dinner partner, making notes if necessary.

The next day, you lunch with the sales manager of the hotel. Hear him (her) out; ask intelligent questions. Under the right circumstances, the sales manager could be useful in the future, too.

When you leave Ft. Lauderdale four days later (or better yet, before you leave) after swimming in the ocean and playing tennis and eating good meals, you will sit down and you will write a "generic" story which you will attempt to place for the next few years. A generic type of Ft. Lauderdale story which will appear somewhere again and again so you have tearsheets to send to these people and others.

This is why it is so important that you are industrious, that you "produce" on the cruise voyage described at the beginning of this chapter. I worked several hours every day at sea. I completed three ports-of-call stories mentioning the ship, plus a piece entirely devoted to the vessel.

It is always useful (but not obligatory) to name the local hotels—especially if you stayed in one and liked it. Thus, a 700-word piece about Ft. Lauderdale mentions the Pier 66 Hotel which extended its hospitality. If you write about Estes Park get the Stanley Hotel in; if you write about Colorado Springs, The Broadmoor Resort.

Can your article be objective? Indeed, it can; you are not beholden to a hotel just because it put you up. By the same token, you can also express your enthusiasm about a beautiful hotel.

Naturally, you can also critique a sponsor—but not too cruelly. A particularly stuffy resort hotel can be called "awesome"; a 2,000-room structure "slightly impersonal." If the supper was lousy, you simply abstain from mentioning the restaurant in an otherwise friendly story. Positive mentions can be done, subtly, too, by just dropping the name once.

The alternative—writing nothing about that cruise or about the City of Ft. Lauderdale—means that you can never ask for help from these people again. And you gain no tearsheets this way. Some travel editors have been known to participate in two-week long junkets without doing a story. A freelancer could never get away with this; he depends on the goodwill of the travel industry and word about the exploitation of sources would soon get around.

Actually, the writer is truly obligated to the readers of the travel guide, magazine article or newspaper. Readers expect honest opinions. I was once invited on a highly touted cruise. When I arrived aboard ship, the decks were filthy. For the first lunch, while still in port, the line was serving little finger sandwiches with slivers of bologna on cheap white bread. Not very impressive.

Moreover, my cabin was as small as a broom closet. I'd never seen anything this tiny. I sought out the ship's purser and told him I couldn't stay in this room for fourteen days. I had to produce travel stories, yet the claustrophobic conditions would make it difficult. Couldn't he find a larger cabin? I was told "no way." The ship is sold out.

During the few hours aboard I happened to see several empty first-class staterooms. They weren't sold out. Unfortunately, the writers had to travel in the hold, just over the engines.

So what does one do in this case? I stepped off the uncaring cruise ship and wrote a negative piece. I have so much shipboard experience that I can evaluate a vessel in four hours.

You do have the option to bail out. Naturally, you won't be invited again by the host.

Solo Versus "Fam" Trips

There are two kinds of complimentary trips. One is to travel on your own. This is for individualists. The other is the junket or "fam" trip. It works best for very adaptable people. The familiarization is usually a group affair; you travel with six to thirty colleagues, sometimes including photographers and/or travel agents. The advantage of group travel? Usually good planning and lots of free liquor. Disadvantage? You're a captive audience. You often ride for long hours in a bus. And you might be together with some heavy drinkers.

Some people therefore prefer the solo trip. You tell the national tourist office what you need, what interests you. Arrangements will be made specifically for you. Airline tickets will often be provided. Some countries offer *pension* style accommodations and meals.

Keep in mind that the solo trip isn't for everyone. It could be lonely.

How about taking along a spouse or friend? This is sometimes possible for an established journalist, or for a couple where the extra person has a *proven* record as a photographer and can supplement the writer's work. In this era of tight budgets, however, such offers are rare. In general, the second person will be charged for transportation, which is costly.

I once received an offer to hike in the Black Forest, for story purposes. My solo trip included free-of-charge airline tickets and hotel space. It was made clear, however, that my national tourist office contact expected me to hike totally alone. For seven days. Personally, I preferred to have a friend along. I suggested it to my prospective hosts. My contacts didn't think that it was possible on a gratis basis. I was told that if I wanted company that would be $80 a day, plus $1,000 for another Lufthansa ticket. The alternative was to set out alone. Lone dinners in a noisy *Gasthaus*. Not very tempting. Luckily, I soon received an invitation from another national tourist office that had no objections to a friend accompanying me.

As for "fam trips," you might be wise to get hold of a detailed itinerary before accepting.

I once participated in a group tour of Scandinavia where we covered almost 1,500 kilometers in seven days. We would often arrive at midnight in a town. It was bright daylight because we were so far north, but all the restaurants closed because of the late hour. We lived mostly on reindeer sandwiches from the train's automat. The invitation, "See Scandinavia by Train," had sounded great. But the reality was not.

Group travel can be unpredictable. The young, the adventurous, the unspoiled are able to adapt themselves to the conditions. I also remember another European junket where everything was regulated as though the military were supervising us. We had five-minute bathroom breaks. The day began with a breakfast of stone hard rolls at 6 A.M. We raced through much of the land by tour bus, seeing too much. Just a small area would have been better. Instead, we visited 800 square kilometers of museums. In a word, strenuous. There are some wonderful group trips, too, especially if they concentrate on one hotel at a Mexican beach resort.

Editors' Attitudes About Complimentary Travel

Newspaper editors *never* pay the expenses of freelance travel journalists.

At the same time, the same editors often warn you in writer's newsletters or personal notes: "Perhaps you are aware of our strict policy regarding so-called "sponsored," "press" or "comp" trips. We cannot accept travel stories from writers who take such trips, nor from anyone who accepts any sort of free or cut-rate service from any travel provider—hotel, transportation, admission fees, air fare and the like."

In a letter to me, the *Christian Science Monitor* travel

editor makes the same point: "Also, I should mention that our current policy is not to accept stories written by freelancers who have taken a free press trip. The *Monitor* writers do not travel on free trips."

Newsday's Steve Schatt considers that "subsidized travel is tainted. As long as we can steer clear of it, we will." Likewise, the *New York Times* and the *Chicago Tribune* warn writers that stories must be produced at their own expense.

Luckily, some travel editors take a more realistic and understanding attitude: they allow writers to go on subsidized trips. The editor naturally reserves the right to cut out some of the favorable mentions or to delete the airline.

Actually, the "high" standards at some papers are unreasonable for the self-employed writers. Some of the newspapers pay $100 at the most. The $100 hardly covers the cost of a decent hotel room for one night.

Some editors understandably resent all commercial input: "I have just one bit of criticism for you," a longtime travel specialist was told. "Could you make your stories less commercial? Must you mention the airline that got you to Honolulu? Other airlines fly that route, too."

Unfortunately the "others" didn't volunteer a free seat.

The editors often fear that you may not be objective if you travel gratis. In my estimation, a freebie isn't a bribe. A free service can't prevent you from writing honestly. To be sure, the pro has the integrity to remain objective, even in the face of a free ride.

If an editor lays down a no-freebie rule, it's *not* a good idea to try fooling him or her; the experienced travel editor can tell quickly from your text if you paid your own way.

Candor is the best policy, even at the risk of rejection. A *Washington Post* editor leaves the door open: "If a writer accepts assistance from a carrier, attraction, agency, area or government, I expect that he will not make any binding agreement (either orally or in writing) to produce specific material on a specific subject and will thus remain free to write or not to write as the case warrants. If the writer has accepted free accommodations or free transportation, please inform us. I also expect that the writer will not agree to give to the donor of the 'freebie' the right to review, clear or edit his article before it is submitted to this market."

An outdoor editor who is also a freelancer paints a fair picture of the overall situation. In a talk to a writer's group, he said: "Of all, journalists, outdoor writers, and travel writers may be guiltier than most of taking—and even generating—special favors. As often as not, it's a matter of simple survival. I can't imagine a freelance travel writer being able to make it without substantial cost breaks for travel, lodging, and services that are, in whole or in part, 'freebies.' Magazine payment rates are rarely commensurate with extensive travel expenses, and not many magazines give adequate expense advances to nonstaffers. Nor can the slack be taken up with income tax deductions. A freelancer's only option is to take advantage of every possible cost break, up to and including freebies."

Working with PR People

In your day-to-day work with PR people, ideally, of course, you are being asked whether you want to go on a trip. The public relations donors know you, have seen your stories. Most PR officials for popular destinations or busy carriers require, however, that a writer have a firm assignment in hand before they will offer complimentary services.

In the majority of cases, however, you have to ask them. If so, you need to put yourself into their shoes. They have to show results from the give-away. A public affairs VP for an international airline spells out his rules: "We go by the track record," he says "and it depends a great deal on how actively we are trying to promote a place. We make a decision, sometimes negative, sometimes positive. If we're trying to promote Timbuktu, it may be positive.

"Sometimes they approach us, sometimes we approach them. If they're going over to research a story, to explore an area of England, Scotland or Wales not over-exposed, we'll listen. We do what we can to expedite things, see that they meet the right people and get to the right sites. Hopefully, they will write a story that will make the reader want to see those areas."

A tourist officer for a Canadian province adds: "In recent years, we have tightened the rules. We welcome freelancers but they must be able to show us a *written assignment* from one or more editors." This assignment clause is popular these days; it hurts freelancers.

Some PR officials are superbly organized; they make all the arrangements at least six to eight weeks prior to your departure. No unanswered questions. Tickets on time. Publicity photos and press material sent beforehand. Every detail taken care of.

Unfortunately, these experts are in the minority. More and more publicists have become sloppy. Your itinerary, your tickets arrive at the last moment. (If part of the airline fare is to be paid by you, the delay prevents you from getting the cheapest rate.) In some cases, promises are made. Yes, there will be at least one free meal a day. Yes, a rental car has been reserved at the airport; the tourist office will pay for it. But no one at the restaurant (or the car rental office) knows about these arrangements. The mystery is never solved. So you dig into your own pocket.

Sometimes you deal with government people who are not as efficient as, say, the Germans or the Swiss. One travel writer, who now lives in a small western town, received an invitation from the Greek government a few weeks ago to fly to Athens. He told his wife, "I am heading for Greece over the weekend."

He was just waiting for his documents, his ticket, his schedule, his itinerary. He waited and he waited. The Greeks said they sent it, not by air mail, but with a courier which didn't deliver promptly in southern Colorado. In any case, the documents arrived three days late. The whole tour was only five days. So he still sits in the Colorado snow, cursing.

Also be prepared for very fussy PR contacts. Some airlines are extremely demanding. An international carrier provided a ticket to Europe; after the writer supplied a written story, the airline PR person expressed serious discontent: "You mentioned us," he said "but you didn't tell your readers that we offer wider seats and more leg room than our competitor."

Another airline—a domestic one—showed no gratitude when a writer supplied a published story which praised the little-known carrier's flight attendants, food and free drinks. Indeed, despite such accolades, the PR person never returned phone calls or answered mail. When the newspaper contributor finally got hold of someone at "Little Known Flights Inc.," he was told that he'd get no further tickets. Reason? His newspapers were in cities where "Little Known Flights" had no gateways.

On occasion, commitments are totally forgotten by your contact and when you phone them with a reminder, no one is there to take the call. (Unreturned calls are a bane in the business.)

You might also keep in mind that a "free" airline flight could mean a "pass" instead of a confirmed ticket. It means that you only get on if they have space. I flew on a "pass" to Casablanca, for instance. But upon trying to return to the United States on the twice-a-week flight, I found that dozens of airline people all waited to board. The jet could only take a limited number of us. So we were told, "You writers stand in the back, please. Regular passengers come first. Then the airline people. The writers come last."

It took four hours of standing and high anxiety. Would we get on? I'd been in Morocco for about ten days and was weak with dysentery. A gruelling situation.

I finally garnered a seat.

Not all freebies are glamorous or even sure.

On the other hand, writers are no angels, either. PR people complain about freelancers who call or write at the last minute and then expect immediate action. ("We're deluged," says one manager; "give us time.")

The IRS and the Travel Specialist

Naturally, even under the best circumstances, the travel journalist incurs unforeseen expenses for taxis, trains, limousines, buses, phone calls, ferries, a dentist, drinks. Some writers pay their own hotels, fearing that strings may be attached to freebies. And there is always the odious ever-more expensive postage and the costs of typing.

In short, you are likely to lay out some of your own funds to produce a travel story or guidebook material. Ditto for your office expenses.

The big question then arises for the newcomer: Are your expenses tax-deductible?

The answer is a definite no for the amateur who merely hopes to sell his output and so far has not received any checks for his writing. The same applies to the person who travels to Italy, for instance, to work on an Italian travel guide which he/she hopes to sell in due time.

The Internal Revenue Service also takes a dim view of enterprises that cost thousands of dollars and then bring one check of $50, for example. Such deductions will be disallowed. In the IRS's eyes, yours has to be a business, not a hobby. In short, the tax people expect profits, not losses, at least from the new travel journalist. (The longtime pro can get away with some unprofitable years if he/she did well during some previous years.)

Beginner or expert, a detailed diary of expenses has to be kept, with lots of legitimate receipts for the expenses and ledgers for your income. I personally save even the smallest professional expense receipts, say $1.00 for a few manuscript envelopes or $3.00 for a snack during a work-related trip.

I employ a bookkeeper to record my many (all honest) expenses and a CPA, who formerly worked for the IRS, to compile my tax return. The alternative? You could study the complicated, constantly changing and tightening laws your-self—something I consider impossible because my time is spent diligently at the typewriter.

This leads to another important point: detailed records must not only be kept for your expenses. You also need to save documentation relating to your work output. The latter isn't always very impressive for the novice who thinks that a travel article a month is enough. Not so. If writing is your business, you really need to prove a hefty daily production. How many stories or words? Your CPA will tell you or you can consult the IRS.

If you work hard enough, you should be able to get some free trips. As one writer puts it: "You might as well travel—it's the best benefit of this job!"

6

Writing Short Travel Features for Newspapers

Why Newspapers Offer the Most Chances for Novices

Now you are thinking about publication. Where should you turn? Newspapers, magazines or books? All come with advantages and disadvantages.

For the beginner, it is easiest to gain a foothold in *small* newspapers. To start with, it is best to forget about the *New York Times, Washington Post, Los Angeles Times, Chicago Tribune* or the *Christian Science Monitor*. Think modestly. Why so? A quick acceptance, and not rejection, probably awaits you at a hometown paper catering to a population of, say, 50,000 or fewer. A small daily or weekly is unlikely to have a regular travel section, so the feature editor may be amenable to running your travel column now and then. You could also try to persuade a friendly suburban paper that you have some interesting stories to tell.

Moreover, there are specialized newspapers, for singles,

for senior citizens, for the sports and outdoors crowd, where your first literary efforts may find a home. *Nota bene:* You won't get rich here. But you will get published and that encourages you to keep writing.

In due time, with patience, you will move up to major newspapers. At that juncture, you can even sell the same piece to a travel section in Boston, Kansas City, Atlanta, Denver, Toronto because these papers, and many others, have no objections to the same story appearing elsewhere. The newspapers are all in different locations with different audiences. So your income from one writing effort can increase.

The newspapers are out there. But there is also a great deal of competition in the field. Editors who publish two freelance articles on a Sunday, in addition to all the "canned" writing that comes in as part of a wire service package (Associated Press, New York Times Service, Reuters, etc.), will be receiving perhaps two hundred manuscripts that same week from which to choose two. So you have to be very good to catch their attention. Do not query; just write your article and send it without a cover letter.

In some cases, your success depends on your originality, savvy, and vivaciousness. How are these determined from the written piece?

Recurring Types of Articles

Lucky is the travel writer with a whole universe for a subject: you can write about villages, cities, states, provinces, the character of entire countries, the people you encounter, the transportation—freighters, ferries, buses, trains, car rentals, even RVs—that get you there, or around. With the right friends, you can write about your yacht trip, Tiffany's & Company or Bulgari Jewelers of Manhattan, the supersonic jet, or eventually, the tourist rocket to the moon. Mayan temples and museums make worthy topics; so do unusual holidays, and how to get along with United States (or U.S.S.R.) Customs.

The exciting foreign cities, like Bangkok or Singapore, lend themselves to good articles. Now the focus narrows and becomes practical: Which type of feature sells well?

There are certain categories that crop up in every travel section weekend after weekend. As you get your own ideas—and you should by now!—you might compare them with the following article groups.

The Service Piece

What is a service article? It is a piece on, for instance, how to obtain a passport. It's an article on how to get a visa, with a word about the visa hassles in France, for instance. Other perennial possibilities:

- Getting the best airfares
- How to travel with a minimum number of suitcases
- Taking better vacation pictures
- What to do when airlines "bump" you
- Hotel discounts for seniors
- How to size up a travel agency
- All about airport-to-town transportation
- What to do in a medical emergency abroad
- How not to become a thief's victim
- Tax laws affecting travel

Likewise, service articles often concern oceangoing vessels. For instance, how to pick a cruise ship. How to tip. How to fly free or cheaply to your port of embarkation.

These 600- to 700-word pieces help guide the reader. Such good advice opens editorial ears and checkbooks, too.

Service articles are simply written, to the point, practical and helpful. A style sample from my own story files:

> Not all ships were created equal, however. Among the ninety vessels that ply the North American waters, some give you more value at a lesser cost than others. So how do you choose?

Here's some candid pointers from an aficionado of the "good value" ocean vacation:

Ask your travel agent about free or reduced flights; air/sea packages are always a better deal for those who don't live near a port city. A typical example? Some cruise lines pay part of your airline ticket to the point of embarkation. You can also ask your travel agent about promotional air fares in connection with other cruises. (It is best to buy your cruise and flight at the same time.)

Wise shoppers do not accept an agent's first suggestion. Research pays off in savings and in a good time at sea. Because cruise brochures all look essentially alike, you might ask some friends, acquaintances or co-workers about their experiences.

The Newsmaker

News articles are popular, too, because no newspaper can send a reporter everywhere; thus, an alert freelancer comes in handy.

The traveling public is hungry for information about new tourism developments.

Examples?

A new, spectacular bridge, a long-awaited tunnel, a causeway to an island all make valid news stories. You might know about a new super-hotel opening its doors in your area. Or four new restaurants that started in business on Wall Street last week.

You can probably sell a short article on the current status of the "Love Boats." What are these cruise ships up to now? Are there new ports of call, new specialty cruises such as forthcoming Western Music or Theatre and Film voyages? (A good travel agent will know some details; you could also report about several lines and their plans.)

The development of Manzanillo, Mexico, and the Las Hadas Resort there, proved to be a welcome news story in its time. The Mexicans regularly build new resorts; just think of Cancún or Ixtapa, which kept many travel journalists busy.

The Update

An update story is still another possibility. It is a difficult story for the newspaper to get because editors can't afford to assign reporters to check up on what's become of Switzerland's famous Zermatt resort, for instance (or other faraway places). But you happen to return to Zermatt after a ten-year absence, to discover so many new hotels and building cranes that you can hardly see the famous old Matterhorn mountain any longer. You could take the same updating approach to Sun Valley, Idaho, or the Florida Keys, or London, or Calgary one year after the 1988 Winter Olympics. Many editors will, however, assign nearby vacation areas to themselves.

To be sure, updating takes some knowledge of a locale and its history. Consider Colorado's large ski resorts, for instance. I keep track of the Vail Resort every few years, cataloguing the many positive changes, the new summer attractions and the new *teleferiques* (gondola lifts) and trails for the winter sports aficionados. Each update will be of interest to editors and readers.

An astute writer could return to the famous Calgary Stampede in Canada for a fresh look. Do the cowboys still drink as much as they used to? Do they still smoke a lot of cigarettes, or do they chew tobacco instead, or nowadays do neither? Is Calgary tamer now? What are the purses for the riders this year? What countries do the visitors come from?

The travel journalist needs to build up files—large files!—for future updates. The mechanics of this are simple but must be consistent: You clip any reference to your topic from newspapers, magazine articles, new brochures, official press kits. I even rush to my notepad if a pertinent area is mentioned on a television program or on radio. The above does not mean that you copy any of your collected materials verbatim; you merely use facts and figures when you get ready to visit the region and write your article.

Keep the update in mind!

The Roundup

What's a roundup article? In this case, you write about several places or subjects at once. Let's say you visit a number of Caribbean islands; if you can find out what's presently going on in Barbados, Aruba, the Bahamas and St. John, you have a roundup article. It costs you money, of course, and saves the newspaper's money. But readers will welcome your roundup because it helps *them* make a choice among the places you describe. You make comparison easy to do.

One travel writer of my acquaintance earns a fair living with columns about several golf resorts in the South or California or New York State or on the island of Maui. Her specialized roundups delight the golfers. In the same vein, I've made money by visiting three or four New Mexico, or Stowe, Vermont or Swiss Engadine ski resorts. In each case, the ski centers lent themselves logically to a roundup story. One might do the same for some New England music festivals, Cape Cod communities or Florida islands. Other ideas:

- The best horse races in the United States
- Three Swiss lakes and their scenery
- The difference between the largest three United States airlines
- Venice, Italy, hotels
- Educational opportunities in Europe
- A tour of Northern California vineyards
- The best health spas in the West

The "Wow" Story

The "Wow" story makes the reader cry out, "How interesting! How unique and different! Wish I could go there!" It might provide a vicarious thrill, a good read. Such a piece doesn't have to be bizarre, but it could be, like one author's repeated visits and descriptions of a Paris cemetery. It should stand out, though, and even surprise the editor. Like, say, a report from a nudist colony.

I returned from Marrakech, Morocco, with a good

"wow" piece about the maddening, complicated city, its noisy markets and too bustling native quarters.

If you have ever been to Cairo, you could come away with a lively description of the insane automobile traffic; after a crash, drivers simply draw apart and go about their business. No police. The dust, the dirt, the dead flies in the museums add to a surprising, yet realistic Cairo story.

Closer to home, an entirely different topic might be unique. Consider an Outward Bound camp for adults, with rock climbing and often daring-do, plus the "solo," during which each participant remains for several days and nights alone in the wilderness. The right kind of harrowing river-rafting expedition, or the excruciatingly slow locomotion in an Old West wagon are unique enough. Archaeology or zoology trips offer exciting possibilities, too.

In short, as you visit a location you must come up with something that penetrates your readers' minds. Any newspaper will be inclined to buy the unique piece designed to make its readers exclaim "Wow!"

The Budget Feature

The budget story inspires the reader's sense of thrift. Most North Americans and Europeans like to save money when they travel. You can make yourself popular by helping your audience get a truly inexpensive vacation. (The word truly here is no accident.)

I recently studied my notes of a recent trip I had taken to Appenzell, Switzerland. The farmers there rent clean rooms to tourists for about $15 a night. And if you are hardy enough to climb higher up you can sleep in a hayloft and pay the herdsman about 5 francs for the night. For that you also get a piece of black bread, a piece of very good Swiss cheese and a fresh glass of milk directly from the cow. Brown cattle keep you company as you enjoy your breakfast in sunny flowered meadows. This is the kind of unexpected information you might provide in a budget story.

If you happen to live in a region that boasts small ski hills without huge resort development (Michigan and Wisconsin come to mind), you could do a short article about the cost-saving aspects of skiing in such places. Colorado, for instance, has Hidden Valley (near Estes Park) and Loveland Valley (near Georgetown) where lift tickets can be had for less than dinner in Denver. You might be sitting on similar stories in your state or province. A typical budget tale can be told about Sipapu, New Mexico; here, a man, his wife and sons operate an inexpensive weekend ski hill, mostly for local consumption.

Inexpensive vacations at certain beaches, in youth hostels or at Club Med copycats are also perfect for the budgeteer. You might be able to come up with bargain accommodations in your city, thanks to some bed and breakfasts, or rooms-for-rent at colleges in summer. You could be "doing" Hawaii on a few dollars a day—an idea that netted Arthur Frommer millions of dollars in book form. European vacationing on the cheap still exists in a few countries, like Yugoslavia or Portugal, for instance.

The Environment Story

Do you visit many national parks at peak summer periods? Then you might be able to do an environment story. A typical one ran in the *Los Angeles Times* and many other newspapers. The topic: the over-commercialization of Yosemite National Park. The writer described how the toilets were overflowing, and how the nights felt "like camping in a parking lot." The park personnel simply couldn't cope any longer with the millions of Fourth of July or Labor Day tourists.

Perhaps you live near another national or state park or too popular picnic camping area that calls out for a similar story. I once exposed the hooligans who tossed bottlecaps into mountain lakes, causing the death of fish. And the vandals who carved their names and hearts into healthy trees. You can find a receptive editorial ear for a story about forest fires, and later, the grey ugliness of the soil—all because of someone's carelessness.

At the same time, a positive nature story still sells. Although she traveled during the nineteenth century through the mountains of the western United States, the Englishwoman Isabella Bird would no doubt be welcomed in contemporary travel sections. She loved the mountains, and she could describe the colors: "Other summits blush under the morning kiss of the sun, and turn pale the next moment; but Longs Peak detains the first sunlight and holds it round its head for an hour at least, till it pleases to change from rosy red to deep blue; and the sunset, as if spell-bound, lingers latest on its crest."

There is a good market for short exploration stories, whether by canoe or raft, on foot or by bike. In these times of rapid change, your audience listens when you offer them a possibility for escape and a slower pace. That's why nature articles are in demand. People enjoy reading about scenic vacations to observe animals whenever they appear in their natural habitat. Stories about the Arctic, the Antarctic, the Galapagos or Seychelles also fit the nature format. Take a whale watching vacation, a photo safari among penguins, helicopter ski adventures in the Canadian Bugaboo Mountains. I was once part of a group following the reindeer across Sweden and Norway; we did it all by train. An editor adds:

"Or it may be a more subtle kind of adventure involving a revealing personal experience in this country or abroad that involves the traveler with natives of the area and results in an illuminating and perhaps moving encounter. Sometimes both types of adventure occur in the same story. In both cases the writer-traveler should seek to transmit to the reader those elements that have added a special dimension to the trip and lifted a vacation above the usual tour level."

Semi-Exposés

Finally there is the exposé.

This is more difficult to place unless you have a big name, are a travel agent or an expert in your own field. On the other hand, a semi-exposé—i.e., a partial critique combined with positive material—might be of interest. The editors rarely dare to upset a major advertiser; for this reason, they think twice before they run a totally unpleasant article about any topic. By the same token, staff writers or writers with clout might be able to get away with a 100% negative story.

Often, a "sandwich" approach solves the problem: you "layer" your article by alternating paragraphs of praise with criticism. For instance: Many Americans are very fond of Las Vegas, and journalists sometimes wear blinders when they report from the gambling capital of the United States. Such an article might be tolerable as a semi-exposé by using the sandwich method. Thus:

> The expanded Las Vegas assaults your eyes evermore garishly. Wild neon lights with marquees blinking out their seductive messages: "Entertainment capital of the world! Fun city! You have truly arrived at this Disneyland for adults."

After stressing some positive aspects about the city, the next paragraph reveals another negative side about Las Vegas:

> Ironically, you wait a long time to catch a city bus from the Strip to downtown. The latter, once modest, is now replete with several waffle iron hotels like the obscenely tall Union Plaza (don't stay there if you need your sleep)."

This article basically shows many interesting and positive sides to Las Vegas. It describes the sports opportunities, the chance to go swimming in all those pools, the free tennis courts and the wonderful climate. The cheap meals, buffet-style, are stressed along with the possibility of renting a car and viewing the desert.

A Miami-based travel writer went on his honeymoon with his young bride on a ship known for its television romances. Unfortunately, the young couple got a cabin with two single beds, army style. He tells about his honeymoon, in good taste, in an intriguing story that combines humor and criticism.

Obviously, a trip to Capetown or Johannesburg makes an automatic exposé; ditto for the red tape in Bulgaria, the rudeness of some natives in the Caribbean and the AIDS danger lurking in some African countries. The *International Herald Tribune* in Paris did an exposé of the greedy, tricky Italian gas stations, which have all kinds of gimmicks to fleece the motorists. The title told it all, "By Autostrada to the Poorhouse."

Timing

When do you write your stories and when should you offer them? You write whenever you can get to a location. This will depend on when you have the time or money to travel, or if you're a professional, if you can get an invitation. The sale comes later.

It's important, however, that you write your article *on location*. This way, it really gets done. At home, other chores await you.

Many newspaper travel sections go by a calendar. They publish European travel at a certain time; their cruise section at a certain date. Regional material, Mexican travel, summer vacations are all assigned fixed dates.

The editor will send you this list upon request. Even certain service pieces, like getting a passport, are tied to the calendar, doing best in spring.

It would be wise to submit newspaper articles at least four to six weeks prior to prospective publication. A summer story arrives too late if you send it at the beginning of summer.

Form and Syndication

Editors generally have certain notions about travel stories. The majority of newspapers prefer short ones because paper, newsprint, and printers' wages are expensive. What's more, readers are always in a hurry and dislike very long articles.

Keep yours to 600 or 700 words. A few papers with large circulations accept 1,000- to 1,500-word in-depth articles. Study the travel pages at a library to see what they want.

Should you write in first person? The answer is generally "no" unless you're a famous author, politician, movie star or travel agent. Exceptions exist, of course, especially in adventure writing. The "you" form is best. Like this:

> If you plan a visit to historical Alexandria, you would be wise to get in touch with the nearest Egyptian consulate or embassy at home; obtain your visa *before* entering the country. A good tip: Exchange only as much money as the Egyptians force you to; keep the rest of your funds in American currency travelers checks. See the blue crescent of the Mediterranean, think of Alexander the Great, of Roman emperors, Greek gods, Arab generals, Napoleon, the Brittons, even silly long-gone King Farouk—all of whom were here, once upon a time, in "Alex."

Most materials lend themselves to a third person approach. This may sound impersonal, but it is effective:

> Fort William, Scotland.—Early Sunday at the foot of Ben Nevis, the pride of the Scottish Highlands: One sees a summer sun as bright as the breakfast eggs. The trail winds and climbs through deep green ferns, past knee-high wild grasses. A few hundred feet higher appears a sudden rivulet. In Ben Nevis's upper region, dark clouds loom.

Rudiments: The Correct Manuscript

Typing has to be flawless, of course. No spelling errors, no grammatical derailments. The manuscript must be triple-spaced, with margins all around.

Your name and address should appear in the top left-hand corner, title CAPITALIZED in the center, about a quarter down the page; on the right, approximate number of words, in hundreds.

In short, the top of your first page should look like this:

Steve Cohen
Box 1930
Durango, Colorado 81301

Travel Feature   Approx. 700 words

SLEEPY PACIFIC PORT AWAKES TO TOURISM

by Steve Cohen

Manzanillo, Mexico.—The name of this tropical city rolls off the tongue as gently as the Pacific breakers that lap at its beaches.

As above, page one of any newspaper travel feature always starts with the location, in this case, Manzanillo, Mexico.

Page two of your manuscript, as well as all other pages, requires your name, or the title of your story (or both, if you wish) on top. On the right goes the page number. Thus:

Steve Cohen   ·2·

Unfortunately, many word processors spew out the page numbers at the bottom which only confuses editors.

Correct this, if you can.

Some manuscripts can now be transmitted by computer. Ask your editor about the technology. Major newspapers, such as the *Chicago Tribune*, will send you instructions.

Here are a few final tips to impress everyone with the "correct" manuscript:

Avoid too many corrections; two or three per page are okay, but no more. Retype. Don't turn in messy manuscripts.

If you're sure about your spelling—of a newly coined word, or a foreign one—you can reassure your editor by flagging it with a circled OK, or a checkmark.

Be meticulous. A single mistakenly spelled museum, street, province makes you suspect in the eyes of the travel editor. Pay attention. Look up every word about which you have the slightest doubt.

Whether you use an electric, an electronic, or a standard typewriter, make sure it has pica type, not elite. The latter is small and disliked by editors who must read many manuscripts. If you use a word processor, you need a letter-quality printer.

Obviously, type faces must be clean. Gummed-up "o's" or "a's" look disreputable; likewise, don't use a worn ribbon or cartridge.

7

The Major Newspaper Travel Feature

How the Professionals Do It

What's the best way to become a pro in this business? Just analyze the short travel stories of professional writers. You'd be wise to do this in the nearest library; recent newspaper travel sections are usually available.

It is not difficult to take a story apart. Ask yourself some simple questions: Did the title give a good clue to the writer's subject matter? What was the lead like? Did the beginning hold your attention? What was the subject matter of the article? Did the writer stick to it? How was the mood created? Where does the pro differ from the amateur?

To save you some steps, here are three sample articles followed by some observations.

1. St. Moritz

Curtis Casewit
P.O. Box 19039
Denver, Colorado 80219, USA

Travel Feature (Based on recent visit) Approx. 900 words

ST. MORITZ REMAINS WORLD'S RITZIEST WINTER SPORTS RESORT

by Curtis Casewit

St. Moritz, Switzerland.—Every winter, some of this planet's most Powerful, along with the Beautiful People, the Jetset, assorted Kings, Princes, Princesses still congregate at this, the Alps' first and most famous winter sports resort. What has changed about St. Moritz? Not much. The industrialists and movie stars arrive with some extra bodyguards perhaps. The Swiss Army and local police have managed to keep out terrorists and other riffraff; roadblocks can be set up in minutes here.

Policed, glamorous St. Moritz sticks to tradition: the Suvretta House, surely the best and most formal of the five-star hotels, still insists that gentlemen patronize the main dining room in a black tuxedo, accompanied by ladies in evening dresses. Most spectators at Prince Charles's winter polo tournament (played on imported Argentinian horses on a frozen lake each January) witness the action in heavy furs. As race horses and their jockeys pound across the snow every February, you spot an occasional elegant male gamble in a lion and leopard coat, plus hundreds of others—and their ladies—in only slightly rarer and less costly furs. From the Corvatsch to the Corviglia summits, most skiers push off not in parkas and ski pants but color-coordinated one-piece ski suits and the latest skis. (You're

stared at in two-year old models.) Even the 370 instructors are clothed in $500-togs by a trend-setting fashion
designer.

This winter's St. Moritz prices are as outrageous as
the stories of the Rich and Famous: Every March, a well-
known German symphony conductor flies to St. Moritz
in his private jet not to ski, skate, hike or party but for a
haircut at his favorite barber. Does beer-heir Heineken
own two chalets? Yes, but the Guccis have six chalets.
(They also sell merchandise in St. Moritz; Cartier and
Bulgari have stores.) You may see well-guarded shipping
magnate Stavros Niarchos at one of the many discos or
King Hussein plus lady skiing with a small, private army
to protect him.

By now, the prestigious resort operates some five
dozen ski lifts in all shapes and sizes, all the way up to
the 2,973-meter Diavolezza and the 3,057-meter Piz
Nair. Tickets are computerized and you can have your
downhill technique analyzed by "video diagnosis." Most
astonishingly, however, St. Moritz leads in its variety of
other winter sports. The visitor can rent hang gliding
equipment, participate (at a price) in an 80 MPH bob-
sleigh run, hitting the curves at Snake Corner and Dev-
ils Dyke Corner, hurtle down the precipitous blue ice
on a Cresta toboggan, or visit one of the thirty curling
rinks. (The St. Moritz Curling Club goes back to 1880;
the club has always been a Canadian favorite.) Ski
joering—skiing behind rented horses—is popular. A winter golf tournament takes place on a frozen lake where
the player is followed by waiters bearing hot tea with
rum against the January cold. The golf ball is red. Some
seventy-five miles of hiking paths are kept sanded for
the many European *Spaziergänger;* cross-country skiers
enjoy one hundred miles of well-manicured trails, plus
helicopter excursions to glaciers. You can watch international ski jumpers, play indoor tennis or swim at the
local *Hallenbad* or, most probably, at your hotel.

St. Moritz now has some fifty hotels plus condos in

fifteen-story high-rises for some 12,000 upscale guests. The five-star Kulm and the friendly Carlton sit on their respective hillsides; the somewhat awesome, gothic-intimidating Palace Hotel is close to everything, including the resort's frantic, breakneck traffic, triple-parked cars and tow-trucks that haul you away. (You're best off to arrive by train with a "Swiss Holiday card" and use local buses.) The ancient Palace Hotel is the place for celebs who want to be seen and for well-heeled vacationers; this winter's average Palace rate is $480 per couple per day. Which buys an incomplete breakfast (eggs extra) and dinner (wine extra). The 230-room Suvretta House is somewhat remote but self-sufficient and aimed at elite travelers who prize privacy, sports (own ski slopes, indoor pools, numerous restaurants, health facilities) and who can get along without disco or rock music. The Suvretta House takes no credit cards; 80% of the clientele are regulars. A few jet in from Gstaad by airtaxi at $710 per one-way ride. (The late Paul Getty once claimed that it was "too expensive" for him.)

To be sure, St. Moritz isn't for economy travelers. Cheap accommodations are scarce here, with *pension* rooms hard to find and generally sold out. (Suggestion: write the local tourist office several months before your Swissair flight touches down at the Zurich gateway; specify your needs in a letter.) Except for a few local eateries at the distant St. Moritz-Bad—and the reasonable Hauser Restaurant in the center of St. Moritz-Dorf—count on laying out beaucoup de Francs for your meals. Shopping? Don't hope for Swiss watch bargains. Avoid the fashion parade at a store cunningly named "Jetset." Bring your own up-to-date ski wear if you can; rent equipment in Zurich or Munich. Expect lift lines, an architectural hodgepodge, beautiful mountain scenery, unexpected skyscrapers, fascinating guests, money thrown around with abandon, in cash, Big Tippers. "Only the sun is free here," goes one local saying.

But you can expect a winter sports resort which has

banished boredom forever. As Hans Danuser, local tourist director, frankly puts it: "St. Moritz is Number One.
We know it. And you know it when you get here."

The lead is straightforward here; it sums up the famous
Swiss resort, tempting the reader with the "planet's most
Powerful" and the "Beautiful People." Indeed, the wealth
and power slant is carried through every page here; you
learn about the costs of the instructors' ski clothes ($500),
and later about the Heinekens (of beer fame), the Guccis
and King Hussein. In short, the theme of the rich and famous emerges and is pursued to the last line, "Only the sun
is free here." In between, take a close and honest look at the
various hotels: the famous Palace Hotel is described *un*-bro-
chure-like as "awesome, gothic-intimidating" and stingy:
"even at $480 a day, the eggs are extra." In the last para-
graph, you're reminded that St. Moritz isn't for economy
travelers. In brief, the theme is maintained throughout the
900 words.

2. Molokai

Curtis Casewit
P.O. Box 19039
Denver, Colorado 80219, USA

Travel Feature (Recent trip)   Approx. 800 words

THE LAST OF THE REAL HAWAII

by Curtis Casewit

Molokai, Hawaii.—Although it takes only twenty minutes to fly here from Honolulu, the island of Molokai
feels remote, rural and tranquil. You might be at the
end of the world. This isle is *slow*. No taxis, no traffic
lights. No fast food chain even. Molokai has no movie

theatre, no elevators, no neons. Development remains minimal. The natives, these true Hawaiians, are afraid of overcrowding.

Molokai's pace is laid-back. When a Type A business traveler, swinging a briefcase, bounded down the stairs of the Hawaiian Air shuttle, the flight attendant told him gently, "Take it easy. Please relax. You're on Molokai!" In all, there're only 6,000 inhabitants who, as local authority Philip Spalding III puts it, "are always waiting for the sunset." The days are pleasant here, thanks to the trade winds. The sunlight picks out the red Hawaiian tulip trees, the reddish soil, the green pineapple fields, the macadamia nut groves. As you drive one of the few local highways, you see a minimalist landscape that reminds one of Africa: gnarled Kiawe trees and pili grasses. Wild boar and deer roam the hills; lots of myna birds and quail, partridge, white egrets along the roadsides. Molokai became King Kamehamena V's favorite island for hunting. Nowhere else in Hawaii do you get such a deep sense of history and legend and native ancestry as on Molokai. Your guide speaks earnestly of Hawaiian gods and goddesses in a melodious language; the curve in the road becomes "nu pu kanla"—"two hills that follow one another." You hike up to a mysterious unmarked boulder field which, you're told, once held a sacrificial Hawaiian temple. Your guide takes you to the far-away house of a local water color painter and past yellow *plumaria* and coconut forests to a herb farm (basil, oregano); both stops consume an hour each as visitors and visited discuss the mango, banana and watermelon crop, friends, weddings, families—an activity which the locals call "talk story."

An important local stable and a remote windsurfing center provide no directions, no signs to get there. A major hotel, the (thin-walled) Hotel Molokai, offers no TV and needs no alarm clocks because all its roosters crow at 4 A.M. On the other hand, where else would you get "Holo Holo Kai" French toast, papaya batter hot-cakes or Hawaiian crêpes with tropical fruit for breakfast?

Molokai doesn't have the massive number of accommodations which you find on other Hawaiian islands. The former 292-room Sheraton is now the (most attractive) Kaluakoi Hotel, complete with an eighteen-hole golf course which overlooks the green and blue ocean. The hotel has two (expensive) restaurants and is managed by the Colony Resorts chain. Among Molokai's condos, David Getchell's friendly Ke Nani Kai units (near the Kaluakoi) provide the most spacious, gracious accommodations in a nest of native orchids and bougainvillea. The $75 to $95 nightly rates mean a good value and utter peace. (Phone: 1-800-367-7040.) The Wavecrest condo complex on the opposite side of the island is less luxurious, with an even lower tariff. A few bed and breakfasts exist, too. (For more suggestions write Destination Molokai Association, Molokai, Hawaii 96757 or call 1-800-423-8733.)

Molokai is one of the islands which has no direct flights from North America. Your Continental Airlines jet takes you only to Honolulu, from where you reach Molokai via Hawaiian Air. Remember that the island has no buses or other transportation, so you need a rental car to get around. On your motorized travels you don't see much other traffic but seatbelt laws are enforced. The scenery of high wooded mountains, waterfalls, green bean and onion farms, alternating rocky or sandy beaches is never monotonous; the few communities—little Maunaloa with its rusty corrugated iron roofs, or Kaunakakai, with its one grocery store and bakery—haven't changed much in the last fifty years.

While essentially still undeveloped, Molokai also has the reputation of being a place without much to do. Not so. You can sail the silvery Pacific on the *Sea Verse II*, a charter boat. You can visit a wildlife park with 500 animals that include giraffes, kudus, oryx. The Big

Wind Kite Factory in Maunaloa gives kite demonstra-
tions. Tennis players enjoy the courts at the Ke Nani Kai
complex. Campgrounds and handsome tranquil picnic
areas are plentiful. Helicopter rides (a bad idea) became available several years ago. You can also go on the
famed "Molokai Mule Ride" seven days a week, all year
long, down and up switchback trails, along with the
"skinners" and European tourists. The ride traverses
rain forests with views of cliffs and the ever-present
ocean below. The six-hour excursion requires strong
legs and $65 per person; it is obviously a gold mine for
the mule owners. During the rest stops, you can, as the
natives put it, "talk story." You hear about the leprechaun-like Molokai *Menehunes*; you're told about the legend of a girl "who turned into a rock."

You depart with the certainty that Molokai is special—the last of the real Hawaii.

The Molokai story is one of my favorites. It deals with
the environment; previous chapters already retraced my research step by step. What can the newcomer learn from
"The Last of the Real Hawaii?" For one thing, travel writing
is always *specific*. I establish my theme by introducing a different Hawaii ("Slow. No taxis. No traffic lights. No fast food
chain"). I focus on the abundant flora and fauna ("red tulip
trees, pineapple fields, macadamia nut groves, pili grasses,
boar, deer . . ."). The Hawaiian motif is kept up with Hawaiian words ("nu pu kanla—two hills that follow one another,"
"leprechaun-like Menehunes").

Even the most nature-conscious feature needs some
nuts and bolts material and a few dollar signs that give the
reader an idea about costs. This piece is no exception. I
mention hotel rates and provide some addresses to write to.
The last page also concentrates on practical aspects, i.e., the
activities on Molokai.

3. Denver's Elegant Restaurants

Curtis Casewit
P.O. Box 19039
Denver, Colorado 80219

Article   Approx. 800 words

THE SURPRISING, VARIED WORLD OF DENVER'S ELEGANT RESTAURANTS

by Curtis Casewit

When people think of Denver, they think of Colorado's high mountains, of national parks, of deep conifer forests and silvery rivers rushing toward the plains. Yet Denver, gateway to the state's tourist wonders—and the Business Capital of Western United States—has also become one of America's restaurant capitals. Gastronomic fireworks in the Mile High City! Epicurean delights, ethnic cuisines! Gourmet hideaways, French haute cuisine—Denver has them all now. Gone is the "cowtown" reputation: an estimated 2,000 local eating places serve a surprising variety of food. And behind the scenes— some fascinating restaurateurs with their own personalities, biases, styles.

For instance: consider the Chateau Pyrenees at 6538 S. Yosemite Circle, off Interstate 25, near the Denver Tech Center. This neo-Baroque gourmet castle is owned and meticulously run by Conrad Trinkaus, an Austrian aristocrat who knows how to create Old World atmosphere: Step down the carpeted staircase under chandeliers, past the classical pianist, past the French Impressionists on the beige walls, to the red roses on your table. Enjoy! French chef Georges Mavro is a master of the delicate avocado soup, the duck consommé with truffles, the roast baby squab, the tournedos or veal medallions, a *ragout de Homard* and many more. Despite Mr. Trinkaus' presence, the service is somewhat slow, however; so allow time as you would in France. Entrée prices? Less than $20 per person; the wines and champagnes are extra, of course. The Chateau Pyrenees is a charmer with groups who relish the intimacy here. Reservations essential (770-6660).

The Wellshire Inn at South Colorado Boulevard and Hampden actually consists of seven dining rooms in a baronial British setting. Leo Goto, the serene owner, first made a name for himself in town at the Westin Cosmopolitan Hotel. His $3 million Tudor style inn overlooks the pastoral scene of a 140-acre golf course and you see the Wellshire's gables from far away. The ancient stained glass windows, an onyx bar, Tiffany lamps and sparkling silver add to the elegance here. The menu is as large as it is versatile. Begin with tempura tidbits or baked Brie Almandine, a stuffed artichoke crown or lox and then proceed to one of a dozen entrées that include marvelous herb-flavored rack of lamb, fresh fish with ginger, Leo's Luau, or a trout Grenobloise. The per-person tariff—$10 to $20 plus drinks—is a good value. In recent years, the Wellshire has added breakfast and lunch service, too. Reservations: 759-3333.

For a centrally located checkered tablecloth-type of French country bistro, you might try the Normandy, at 1515 Madison, not far from the airport. Like many of its counterparts in Europe, the Normandy is owned and supervised by a man and his wife: The Gerstlés are always on the premises, knowing and greeting their guests, discussing the newest dishes. Any wine suggestions? Ah, M. Gerstlé is the right person to ask! The Normandy proprietor often travels to the vineyards, personally inspecting the output of the best California and European estates. The lunchers and diners—locals and tourists alike—seem a bit noisier than elsewhere; maybe it's mix of acoustics and the casual atmosphere that increase voice decibels here. The customers are attacking the crunchy French bread, the real article, and digging into their appetizer plates of paté campagnard. Other guests are eagerly setting their forks into an *escalope de veau Marie Antoinette*, the most seductive of veal cutlets with fresh mushrooms, a burgundy sauce, Parmesan cheese. The Normandy is usually jammed. So call ahead (321-3311). Rates compare with the other better restaurants.

Finicky business travelers and tourists lodged at downtown hotels don't have far to go for one of Denver's finest meals. No farther than the sleek Augusta Room at the Westin Hotel, 1672 Lawrence Street (572-9100). Every table has a dazzling view of Denver's many new sky-scrapers—a tableau of bright lights at night. The tuxedoed waiters are friendly, despite the Haute Cuisine of duckling mousse, herbed snail in cream, the lamb sweetbreads, the Canadian goose *cassoulet*; for dieters, the Augusta Room excels in rotisserie dishes and "Healthmark" items. The presentation is straight out of *Gourmet* magazine. And even the wines by the glass come from France.

Which are some other Denver "in" restaurants? The Rattlesnake Club at 901 Larimer (573-8900) features sophisticated, imaginative American cooking; the dishes here are intriguing and many-hued, all at very high prices and with city views. Churchills, at the Writers Manor Hotel (1720 S. Colorado Blvd., 756-8877), has a British maitre d'y, English waiters, enormous shrimp cocktails, excellent fresh fish and quail; for dessert, the poached pear in raspberry sauce or the strawberries in Grand Marnier can be recommended; the chef is Dutch. The Quorum, 233 E. Colfax, 861-8686, is still the lively province of multi-lingual Pierre Wolfe. After years of elegant French sauces and large portions, the Quorum now offers a light menu which includes your choice of coq au vin, or braised lamb, or duckling strips, among others, at about $12 per meal.

All of which adds up to progress in a convention city once known as a "steak and potatoes cowtown"— where visitors now spend $5 billion a year.

The above entry is the important "roundup story," i.e., a number of good restaurants in one city. The catchy word "surprising" in the title is meant to arouse the reader's interest. The lead attempts to overcome the average United States Easterner's skepticism about Denver as a "restaurant capital." The story is typical for up-to-date travel writing: your audience demands addresses, phone numbers with area codes, and *detail* ("herbed snail in cream, lamb sweetbreads or Canadian goose *cassoulet*"). Indeed, don't be afraid to season your descriptions with an occasional foreign word; this enriches your material. The last line returns to the beginning, and underlines the thesis that Denver is no longer just a "steak and potatoes cowtown."

4. Down on the Farm

Last, a short effective little travel feature for the *Army Times* newspaper by much-traveled Steve Cohen. Note how smoothly he gets into his story. He wastes no time to establish the theme of this newsy, practical little piece.

He gives precisely the information that one needs about the animals, farming activities, and meals.

Cohen winds up his valuable account with an anecdote. The latter is touching indeed. And fits perfectly into New Zealand's farm life.

DOWN ON THE FARM

by Steve Cohen

There is no better way to meet New Zealanders on their own turf, and on their own terms, than by experiencing a New Zealand farm house and country holiday.

"Everyone loves the farm stay," says Diane Anderson of Air New Zealand's Los Angeles office. "I've seen it every time. There's nothing I can tell you before you get there. Everyone's real nervous. Will they like me? Will it be boring? Then when it's all over you loved it."

It begins when you make reservations through one of several farm stay bookers. You arrive at a pre-arranged point to be met by the hosting farm family. You eye these strangers, just as they eye you, everyone equally nervous.

Then, quickly, after brief introductions are exchanged, you are on your way. You probably pass through numerous sheep fields, called paddocks, or traverse grain fields and woodlots. In this area, situated between the city of Christchurch and the foothills of the Southern Alps, are rolling hills and rivers.

Most of the farm host families are well-to-do and welcome strangers into their homes about once a month for an average stay of two to three days. They host families out of curiosity and an interest in bringing a zest into their homes. How else would a rural New Zealander get to meet Japanese or Canadian or U.S. visitors other than traveling abroad?

On the farm you will probably be served tea in the afternoon and fed well at mealtimes. You could find yourself herding sheep, perhaps with a walking stick while dogs do the herding, or maybe from a car as your farmer host drives slowly behind a flock, wheeling about the paddocks and nudging the sheep this way or that. Bee hives, windbreak woodlots and vegetable gardens are all common on these farms as smart farmers diversify to increase their security. Livestock proliferate—thousands of sheep, cattle and lately small herds of deer. Many of the deer lose their antlers to a growing Asian market in supposed aphrodisiacs.

A farm tour can take you to baling sheds where wool is packed tightly in large bundles, or to a shearing operation. In springtime you may witness a birth.

A farm dinner will usually consist of fresh local meat, likely to be lamb, potatoes, vegetables from the garden, good New Zealand wine, probably a few schooners of beer. Your hard working hosts will bustle around cleaning up and offering solicitous care, along with conversation that tends to start formally and get friendlier as your visit goes on.

You do not have to do a lot to enjoy this sort of holiday. All the farm stay homes are checked beforehand to maintain standards for private rooms and bath facilities. And rest assured that you are wanted. The farm hosts are not obligated to accept anyone, but instead sign up as possible hosts and have the option of saying yes or no to a visit.

For your part, you get to see and meet these people in their homes, the least pretentious setting for visiting anyone and the best chance you have to get to know them.

Intimacy develops quickly. Whether you get out and help in the fields or just watch, once you sit around someone's dining table and break bread there, perhaps sip some wine or toss down a few beers, for all intents and purposes you are a part of the family. It is a great way to start a friendship.

One farm guest who had stayed only one night on a farm near here was surprised when, a week later, while at the airport in Christchurch to catch a flight back to the States, his farm hostess and her teen-age son were there at the terminal waiting to say good-bye.

The guest had forgotten an inexpensive traveling clock and they had driven 50 miles to return it. They had also brought a bottle of homemade "mead," honey wine, along as a going away gift. Needless to say, the guest was touched deeply by this kindness in a way he will long remember.

Contact your travel agent for complete details on New Zealand's farm stay holidays.

How to Create Mood and Ambience

A travel story will succeed if it reflects a sense of place, the mood or ambience, the sights and sounds and smells of a destination. The reader has to feel the magic, and it's your job to conjure up all the right elements. These include shapes and colors. Example? Watch Kate Simon, that great word painter, at work in Rome:

"A gentle pale-blue canvas of sky—medieval houses melting on each other in mutual support, zigzags of red tile and green terrace running together to greet a church steeple. . . ." Bravo! *Bis!* More!

In all her travel guides, Kate Simon's work transports us, trills the purest, modulated arias, awakens marble statues, whisks us to the gushing fountains on Piazza Navona at night, "the essential experience."

She always brings a place alive; so does Paul Theroux who writes, "As I came down, the wind would blow me a vista open through which I could see the country eastward, boundless forests and lakes and streams gleaming in the sun."

Truman Capote visited Tangier, to describe it as "hemmed with hills, confronted by the sea, and looking like a white cape draped on the shores of Africa."

The sense of place comes easily to some writers, even total novices. A young woman, one of my family members, who has no intention to be a travel journalist, wrote us about a visit to Budapest:

Round-faced peasant women sold paprikas and red peppers in vegetable stands and also lovely fruits. Many people rode bicycles and, although there were some cars, it wasn't as frantic as western Europe. Hungary is very flat, and on the radio one could hear gypsy songs; many people really have those tribal, gypsy features. We could easily imagine them roaming in caravans across the plains as gypsies before the Communists came.

Another time, she and her husband came upon a Saudi Arabian desert settlement that goes back to antiquity. Her descriptive letter home can teach many of us a lesson in mood.

> Suddenly, there in the distance behind a pitted ridge of lava stone shone a lush mass of date palms and rising beside them we could make out the semi-fortified mud houses of the ancient township of Khaybar, north of Medina. As we approached, the dimensions of the large oasis became apparent. High stone walls encircled the intensely cultivated plots of land under towering trunks of well-tended palms. But where were the people? Khaybar stood virtually abandoned! We saw row upon row of heavy-set buildings made of mud, palm trunks and coarsely hewn stone, all of them uninhabited and many giving way to the elements. How mysteriously quiet it was! Only the sound of birds interrupted the perfect silence.

Obviously, talent plays its part here. Gifted writers make us *see* a place.

First-rate editors demand such prose from all contributors. If they fail, they may get an editorial reminder like this one: "There's almost no sense of character and flavor, especially reflecting someone's on-the-scene reactions. You've basically written this in machine-gun fashion, firing short factual bursts at us."

Unfortunately, the run-of-the-mill writers make no attempts to set a scene. A recent issue of a newspaper for seniors ran an Alaska piece in 500 words that told us about Mt. McKinley ("the highest mountain in North America"), Anchorage ("a modern city"), Sitka ("once the capital of the Russian fur empire") and so on. Not a single image. Not one real sight. Total lack of observation or freshness. The author gave us a few platitudes and never showed us Alaska.

Good writing comes with experience. Even the pro revises and polishes, however, and the newcomer must truly throw himself into the task of improving a manuscript. Is it worthwhile, considering the modest financial rewards? Actually, polishing is essential lest you be rejected. And publication brings more than just money.

Most beginner's articles come with many flaws. "Cooling" the article is one way of seeing it anew. After a few days, you can re-read it. Suddenly, you notice repetitions, redundancies, impossibilities, illogical points, even lack of clarity.

Now you can rewrite the piece successfully.

Irreverence

You need not rave about every travel destination. A little irreverence has its place in a story, too. Not long ago, a writer focused on a woman who owns many major hotels, how she lives and how wealthy she is and how she deals with her staff. The piece was candid and couched in humor.

The author wittily shows that the lady is difficult to work for. After badgering and hassling her entire staff, she declares:

"'I'm taking off to Palm Beach with my gorgeous husband,' she announces. Spirits begin to lift.

'But for two days only, don't get excited.'"

Irreverence can be used by restaurant critics to good advantage. Gael Greene, of *New York* magazine, does especially well with her subtle humor. After reviewing a French-owned Manhattan hotel in great detail, she concludes:

"In all, our night at the Hôtel Plaza Athénée cost $474.48. If I weren't blissed out on raspberries and the $474.48 were coming out of my bank account, I think I would picket the place."

All About Photographs

It must come as a surprise to most novices but it's true: all newspaper editors expect photographs with every travel story. *You* are supposed to procure these pictures, yet you seldom get paid for them.

Most newspapers use black & white 8 x 10 or 5 x 7 glossy shots; these pictures need to tie in with the subject in your manuscript. Some travel editors want quality color photography; if necessary, they convert color slides to black & white. Fortunately, most papers don't care whether these illustrations are first-class or not. The powers-that-be know that they are lucky to get the photo material free of charge.

Should you run out with your 35-mm camera and start shooting? Only if you want to, and if you can afford it. Developing (and blowing up) black & white film has become costly; your expenses to furnish pictures to thirty or forty newspapers will cut deeply into your writing profits. Some newspapers use color slides; color film and processing of transparencies aren't cheap, either.

Logical solution? Get hold of some *free* pictures. You can obtain the latter en masse from the travel industry. But you should learn how to evaluate what you get and send an editor good pictures only.

Specifically, you can write to:
- State tourist departments
- Hotel chains
- PR departments at resorts
- Cruise lines
- Museums
- Corporations
- Associations
- National tourist offices
- Airlines

While researching a story, you may want to find out which local agency can help you with gratis illustrations.

Naturally, if you are an amateur photographer, as well as a writer, you will want to take some of your own pictures. Good ones can be sold to all kinds of outlets apart from newspapers. For market leads, and advice regarding photography, contact the *Photoletter*, in Osceola, Wisconsin 54020.

Editors like to see the pictures with a manuscript. Keep in mind that you are expected to identify the subject in the photo. This takes captions.

Photo Captions

Your style can be simple, and the information need not exceed two lines. But it should be to the point. The purpose of captions is to identify people, objects and events in your pictures.

You can type captions on strips of paper which you paste on the backs of your 8 x 10 glossies. (Typing directly on a photo may ruin it.) Some freelancers prefer to use a separate letter-sized sheet to explain the subject of a dozen or more shots. It's easier to make a carbon this way. (Most editors prefer this method over the other, also.) Example? When *Grit*, a newspaper for small town readers, requested some Christmas pictures, the caption sheet read:

1. A few more days of school, but soon it's Christmas!
2. The snow-covered logs are piled high to last through another family gathering around the fireplace to celebrate the Christmas season.
3. A glistening and shimmering small-town Christmas Day.

Captions should entice the reader. They should contain an element of surprise. After all, most people just look at pictures. This way you get them to read, too.

Photo agencies which service many papers and magazines sometimes want you to write directly on the 35-mm slide mount or on a narrow slip of paper that can be affixed to the mount. More guidelines? Put your information on one edge of the slide frame. Use the other edge for your name and address label. (Unless you do this, valuable pictures can get lost at an office.) Always print neatly, of course. Some photographers use tiny rubber stamps to identify their work. Your name is an important part of the credit line which indicates ownership of the photos. Bear in mind that few newspapers will credit you for your pictures; on the other hand, magazines do.

Naturally, even good photos are not enough. You also need a good travel feature or article.

One journalism professor puts it this way: "Writing is like pulling the trigger of a gun. If it's not loaded, nothing happens."

Where to Get Sales Leads

For most writers, it is a thrill to see their byline in print for the first time. Ah, you can share a travel experience with the world! You're an author!

Actually, authorship also implies payment. It needn't be much at first, but ideally, there should be a check. Professionals think in terms of checks, plural. They submit to many newspaper travel sections at the same time. This way they (or you) can get multiple payments.

How do you get started in marketing?

Begin with some market research. Find out who is buying. Where could you go with a 600-, 700-, 800-word article? Research is well-invested time. Start with the local news vendors, whether you win any popularity contests or not. Look at the Sunday papers at any major newsstand, also at your airport. Study each travel section. How long is it? How many pages? Are there freelance writers? If they are staff writers it generally says so under their names. Does the travel editor regularly write the whole section? Then you might as well forget about that paper. You're wasting your time by sending manuscripts. If you see only syndicated writing week after week, you won't have a chance, either. Some newspapers use one or two freelance pieces every Sunday. This means competition but you might get in. Some larger newspapers like *The Boston Globe* or the *Los Angeles Times* run numerous freelance stories every week. Here's your opportunity.

For a more leisurely and more thorough study, head

for the nearest university library and the main public library downtown. Go to the newspaper section which has about twenty to sixty papers. You don't read the entire Sunday section, of course.

You can't amuse yourself. Forget the tempting crossword puzzles. Concentrate on the travel section. Take it out and analyze it from one end to the other, including the ads. Lots of cruise advertising? The editors can be influenced to do a cruise story. You'll have an immediate sale because it ties in well.

Sunday papers are available three to four weeks back. The current Sunday isn't enough. Try the last four, even the last six, if you can.

How long are the stories? 500 words? 700? 1000? Do they come with color pictures or black & whites?

Making Contacts

The travel section should also yield the name of the travel editor. He or she will be usually identified at the top of a column. You need to address your manuscripts to this individual. Next, how do you obtain newspaper addresses? Ask your librarian for the latest *Editor & Publisher Yearbook*. This large, invaluable volume lists every newspaper in America; it also tells you who is the current travel editor. (If you write about music, the *Yearbook* gives you the name of the music editor; ditto for business, entertainment, women's pages and other departments.)

You can also obtain good leads from the yearly O'Gara's *Travel Writer's Markets* list (see details in the bibliography). Here you get details about many American and Canadian buyers.

The Canadian market is often ignored; yet these friendly newspapers use some bylines from the United States. True, you will be paid in Canadian dollars, which are worth less than ours. But the editors are often gracious and always aboveboard; they won't run your pieces and then not pay you. Indeed, the Canadians are honorable people, and you will find it a pleasure to do business with them.

Moreover, their travel sections span a continent, from Vancouver to Toronto and all the way from the Yukon down to Saskatchewan. In Toronto alone, there are four prospective papers.

To Market, to Market!

Getting hold of and studying possible leads actually saves you time, allowing you to avoid people who chronically refuse to use freelancers. Get your literary feet wet; start submitting as soon as possible to the most likely papers. Some good writers procrastinate too much and thus never see their byline in print. If you are shipping out a manuscript to some twenty to forty Sunday travel sections, you can call it "self-syndication." This sounds impressive; realistically speaking, it means that you spend a lot of money for postage. (The post office generally makes a big profit on writers.)

In case you're wondering, your doublespaced manuscripts can be originals or perfect photo copies. Mail them flat, with one or two photos. You need no cover letter. Your story speaks for itself.

Keep in mind that newspaper travel editors want to see the actual manuscript from the average contributor. Queries? Forget about them unless you are a top pro, and the paper is familiar with your byline and style. Newspaper assignments are rare in the travel business; most submissions simply come "over the transom," i.e., unsolicited through the mails.

Could you get some marketing help?

It is virtually impossible to interest a major national syndicate in short travel features. The giant syndicates use their own regular contract writers; most of them are newspaper travel editors or travel section staffers. Freelancers are seldom considered.

Nor are there literary agents who sell newspaper stories. (Agents prefer to represent book authors.)

So be prepared to do your own selling. Ideally, you will try to reach one paper in many major cities. For this reason, it's unwise to write a story for only one outlet. If that newspaper doesn't want it, you are sitting on a limb. Think nationally and internationally! Multiple markets—writing universally—is the only way to make it as a freelancer. By the way, no editor minds if your byline appears in another state, province, or country; just don't market the same story to two newspapers in the same community.

What are your chances of breaking through? At first, you can count on lots of rejections. But eventually, some of your stories will stick. To be sure, it depends on the freshness of your ideas and writing; in time, if you are good, maybe every fifth or tenth manuscript will be bought.

Relationships with Newspaper Editors

If you make fifty sales attempts, at least five or so should click. Once an editor accepts your work, hit the iron while it's hot. Submit more, perhaps one a week.

- Don't expect any correspondence.
- Everyone at a newspaper is *very* busy.

Should you visit an editor when you're in his/her city? That depends on a number of factors. The novice had better not do it; editorial time is precious. But once you've sold someone a number of articles and you happen to visit the person's city, you might try a phone call. The editor may then say, "Come and say hello." Or better still: "Let's have lunch!"

It doesn't hurt to nurture such relationships, so long as the writer avoids gross flattery, social invitations ("We're giving a party next weekend. Would you like to come?") or long letters. On the other hand, a postcard from the Seychelles or China does no harm; it shows that you were actually there.

It is easy to upset a newspaper travel editor. One way is to put a ©, or copyright notice, on your stories. Don't do it;

your works are automatically protected.

Will an editor "steal" your idea? In rare cases, he or she may assign the idea to a staff writer who, in turn, will put a personal emphasis, or slant, on it. This happens quite seldom, however.

On the other hand, your travel feature may find its ways into print in a distant city—one of the many to which you sent a manuscript. You may have forgotten that you actually submitted your masterpiece to that particular editor in Oregon or New Hampshire. Suddenly your Aunt Mabel writes. She saw your name in last Sunday's travel section!

You may be concerned that you won't be paid for your work.

What to do?

First of all, try to get hold of the published piece. Maybe Aunt Mabel still hasn't tossed it into the trash. If she has, you may want to wait a week or two; the busy editor will possibly send you tearsheets. If you don't hear from the travel editor, drop a line with a $3 check to the circulation department of that newspaper and ask for a copy of the particular issue with your masterpiece. Or see if a major library in your neighborhood has that week's paper.

By now you've gotten hold of the published feature. What to do next? Don't get angry; the editor may have forgotten, been on vacation, gotten fired or been shuffled to another department. In short, keep calm and don't destroy a possible contact.

Payment always follows *after* newspaper publication. It may take anywhere from two to six weeks to get a check; in some cases, you will know that your financial reward will be forthcoming because the accountants ask for your social security number. Payment runs from $10 to $150 per article.

Do editors run your stuff without remuneration or tearsheets? Yes, it can happen but *very* rarely. If it does, drop a polite cool line saying that you'd appreciate payment. If none is forthcoming, forget about that particular paper. Concentrate on others which *do* pay you. Always try to obtain tearsheets which are worth their weight in gold.

It takes patience and persistence to succeed. Meanwhile, whatever you do, keep the competition in mind. Strive to be better than other freelancers. Aim for outstanding, can't-put-them-down manuscripts. The checks will then follow on their own.

8

Tapping the
Magazine Market

What Makes the Magazine Piece Different from the Newspaper Feature?

The travel writer often graduates from the newspaper feature to the magazine article; the former takes less of an effort and can sometimes be knocked off quickly by a newcomer, an amateur, or someone in the business such as a travel agent. And the magazine piece? In general, you can't just send an article to the better magazines; you should query, which, in turn requires a definite angle or focus. In short, the magazine article must be more sharply delineated and more deeply researched. With a few exceptions, newspapers allow you multiple sales—one per city—while major magazines demand exclusives. A quick little feature for the *Rocky Mountain News* or the *Detroit Free Press* or the *Oakland Tribune* is perishable; you see the travel section in Monday's trashbin. By contrast, a piece in the *National Geographic* will be indexed for researchers and consulted by the public for years. Certain magazines, in sum, give you more prestige than the average tabloid. And of course, by and large, magazines pay better than newspapers. "I have had several offers to do more guides," says one travel writer. "Books take too long. I enjoy the brief *magazine* effort. My average fee is about $800 for a week's work." (For more money details, see end of this chapter.)

What other differences are there between the periodicals and newspapers? The respected monthlies demand unfailing accuracy; indeed, their research staffers double-check your every word and fact. (You should be accurate in everything you write, of course.)

At the same time, especially at better publications, you gain more freedom. The average Sunday travel section contribution can be as short as 500 words, which doesn't allow you much space to create atmosphere or to provide many facts. On the other hand, magazine pieces start at 1,200 to 1,500 words and in some cases, reach 5,000 words, or twenty-two double-spaced, typewritten pages. Even a shorter length— say, ten pages—requires a more complete presentation of your subject matter than a short travel section feature.

Good magazines allow for a variety in style; in fact, you often have an opportunity to write with dash and panache, to really let go, to stick to your own individual tempo. The old, literary *Holiday* magazine (circa 1946 to 1977) permitted article writers to be themselves. Surely, such giants as Faulkner, Steinbeck, Capote wouldn't deviate from their styles when penning *Holiday* travel articles. You still encounter some "names" in a few current issues of *Vogue, Vanity Fair,* and on rare occasions, in *Travel & Leisure.*

All are worth studying and emulating.

Achieving Depth

Newspaper articles—especially by the multi-syndicated writers who must produce them *en masse,* are often superficial. The writer takes a couple of days to evaluate a new place, and depth is sacrificed for copy cranked out after a quick look and see. On the other hand, magazine pieces demand genuine interviews with the local people, a broader understanding of a topic, and even a thorough library study. You can't rely on releases or brochures. You also personally visit the churches, museums, hotels and shops or restaurants on location until you're on sure ground with your subject.

No statement is made from the top of your head; all must be checked out. Depth means knowing a field as Paul Theroux knows trains and William Weaver knows Italian *palazzi*. Depth? I once decided to do a critical article about the gambling frenzy in Las Vegas for a major Christian magazine. Before setting out for the casinos, I proceeded to a good library for a look at what the world's best minds— from Luther to Nietzsche, from Schopenhauer to Wilde— had to say about games of chance, greed and sleepless nights at the *jeux*. My slant was subjective but backed by thorough research: my on-location interviews concerned slot machines and gaming tables, croupiers and security personnel. Result? Two thousand galloping words about financial ruin in Nevada. (The same two Las Vegas trips made it possible to write a spinoff article for *Modern Bride* on the city's honeymoon possibilities.)

Achieving a thorough knowledge means going on not just one but five to ten ocean cruises before attempting a "Why You Should Go On a Cruise" article. The multiple journeys give you better judgment, of course; you pick up details which make your article sound authoritative. Such knowledge has to do with keen observation, too. A few years ago, *Denver Magazine* gave me an assignment. Would I compare Denver's various scattered public tennis courts for their magazine readership?

Many writers would have breezed through the research in a day. Instead, I spent at least two days per public park and court to evaluate the players, the facilities, and the atmosphere. The resulting article showed that I had done my homework.

Article Leads

The magazine travel article is hard to sell without a good beginning—one that grips the reader and editor. Such a lead must be in perfect harmony with the theme and content of your piece. Each publication has its own favorite first paragraphs. A study of four or five back issues will show you the editors' tastes.

Some magazines want you to guide the reader directly into your subject, conjuring up the ambience at once. One typical example comes from the Mexican airlines in-flight magazine. My article started this way:

> Cross the tree-shaded plaza, step into the tourist office and ask what the hectic eighties are doing to the historic town of San Miguel de Allende. "Everything is the same here, Señor," you'll be told. And it is true: this colony for writers and artists, riders and rest-seekers has lost none of its drowsy quality. Despite the super highway which makes the 180-mile drive from Mexico City easier these days, San Miguel has changed very little. The pace is slow.
>
> The San Miguel houses are still strewn over the hillside like pieces of colored candy squares on the street vendors' carts. Donkeys still move across the cobblestones. The church bells ring out as they did more than 400 years ago after Juan de San Miguel, a Catholic friar, founded the town.

The mood and slant are established in these two paragraphs. The reader knows what he/she is getting.

Good magazines sometimes allow you to write in first person; to be true to your material, you need to start out in the "I"-form. I did this in a nostalgic but up-to-date article for a short-lived publication published by the Denver Cen-

ter for the Performing Arts. My *Bravo Magazine* lead immediately painted the local scene:

> After many years of absence, I returned to Montreal for
> a few days. Someone took me to the Place Jacques Car-
> tier and its centuries-old buildings with high chimneys
> and dormeres. The fruit vendors did their colorful com-
> merce. The antique shops bustled. The outdoor cafes
> were full of people drinking aperitifs. The painters had
> propped their oils against ancient stone walls. The
> scene reminded me of a Utrillo street scene of Paris.
> The importance of dining well remains, too. Montreal
> now boasts some 2,000 restaurants.

You will find it enjoyable to differ your beginnings for
each article. Among others, you can choose among the following: *The anecdotal lead* starts with a story—one that illus-
trates the entire article. Here's a typical one I created for
the (defunct) *Progressive Woman* magazine during the seven-
ties. Titled "The West's Fanciest Ski Resorts," it began like
this:

> The place was Sun Valley, the time a pleasant March
> day, the occasion, a ski fashion show. Lovely clientele,
> those slim, tanned ladies from Beverly Hills and Palm
> Springs and even from Palm Beach, Florida, all seated
> against a backdrop of wolverine parkas, fur jackets, seal-
> skin ski coats. And lovely models, flown in for the Idaho
> event.
>
> Nevertheless, the shop owner felt some trepidation.
> Did he have too many ski stretch suits? Too many im-
> ported ski pants?
>
> It turned out that he had too few, for almost every
> one of these fine femmes bought six to eight ski outfits,
> each costing about $300. One vacationer acquired fifty
> sweaters. To this, you must add gold-plated ski poles,
> super-streamlined plastic ski boots (tomato red or mus-
> tard green), ski goggles, ski caps.

Such a lead ties in with the theme of poshness and Big Money in this article; moreover, these three paragraphs can later be used as part of the query letter to the editor. *The startling lead* can be suitable, too: "Buongiorno a tutti!" from a Verona story.

The summing up lead immediately tells you what the article is about, like this piece about working in the French vineyards: "It's an education, an adventure, a way to meet friendlier French people than the tough Parisians. Some very young and very old North Americans have helped with the grape harvests. If you're thinking of the *vendange* (harvest) this autumn, you'd be wise to plan and study the possibilities long in advance."

The dialogue start can work, too. Here's how I started an article about Tucson, Arizona: " 'Good morning! Be prepared for some beautiful weather,' says the eager forecaster on your hotel TV screen. Outside your picture windows, the mauve Santa Catalina Mountains stretch under a flawless blue sky."

Whatever you do, you must capture the essence of a place in that first paragraph. It can be a newsy beginning, or a descriptive one; you can even launch your article with sounds and smells. At all times, you need to give the reader a fair warning what to expect—the humorous or the outrageous or even an exposé.

Establishing a Unique Idea

Before you can create the sales letter to your editor, which is known as the all-important *query*, you have to decide on your slant and somehow create a short outline for yourself. Think of the novelist who first starts with a short blueprint of each chapter, or the motion picture writer who begins with a *treatment*.

In short, you need to get the idea on paper. Thus: A 1,600-word article about Colorado's leading hostelries, especially those that offer skiing. You might include these:

- The Broadmoor in Colorado Springs (its own ski slope)
- The elegant Keystone Lodge at the Keystone Resort (big skiing)
- Tamarron, a plush complex near Durango (its own hill)
- The Hi Country Haus Resort, a condo center at Winter Park (cross-country activity)
- The Sheraton Steamboat, a massive resort hotel in Steamboat Springs
- Beaver Village, a cozy ski lodge cum condominiums at Winter Park (large ski complex)

The focus would be on the above places, but more would be mentioned.

The list helps you to clarify the slant and tell about places you intend to write about; later, you can fashion these notes into a simple query by starting it, "Would you be interested in an article about Colorado's leading ski hostelries?"

Before you pen the actual query, you have to ask yourself a few important questions about the actual travel article idea. Does the planned article inform or enlighten the reader? Do you provide *new* data that, to your knowledge, has never been presented before? Is your idea unique enough to compete with many others hitting the editor's desk? If your suggestion is an old one—say, a piece about Paris—do you have a fresh approach?

Good magazines are picky. They don't need conventional destination pieces. They assign these to their favorite friends. They let staff writers do them, as a reward for long service.

In a classic statement, a longtime travel editor complained that she is always stunned when she gets letters or phone calls from freelancers whose idea of a proposal is the following: " 'I'm going to be in Indonesia, Malaysia and Singapore; what can I do for your magazine?' We call this kind of place-dropping approach 'globespinning' in the office and my first inclination is to say, 'Have a good time and send me a postcard! The name of a destination is not an idea. It is only a geographical identification." Editors naturally prefer the specific to the generalized. They expect an angle from you, maybe on the etiquette and pitfalls of doing business in Singapore; on the cuisine of Malaysia or the climate of Indonesia. Being specific, or having a slant on Paris could mean an article on the American Express Office there, with details on the little-known functions, i.e., bulletin boards, hangout for young travelers, a place for networking or making friends. Paris could inspire a serious study on why the natives are so rude to visitors and to each other, with quotes by worldwide experts on the subject.

One associate travel editor told the members of the *American Society of Journalists and Authors:* "Paris is not an idea. It is a city. 'The wine bars of Paris is an idea' —" In short, there must be a twist, or novelty, or even a whimsical approach. An editor should be startled or intrigued by your proposal. If he/she says, "I didn't know *that*," then you have a good idea.

Basic Selling

There are basically two ways to get into a publication: 1) you write your travel piece, send it in and hope for the best. This works fine with minor or secondary magazines, where only a little money changes hands. Or 2) you phone the editor (which takes courage), 3) or send an intelligent three-quarter or full-page query outlining your idea. The telephone can bring results; in general, though, you will be told to send in a proposal. The latter can be passed around and discussed among the magazine's staff, and then okayed. That's how you obtain an assignment for a magazine. The latter sometimes involves a deadline, the date your editor expects the completed article. Make sure that the deadline is realistic and that you can meet it.

To get some attention, you always need to tell the powers-that-be who you are, and why they should listen to you.

Thus:

• I'm well-qualified to write about Tangiers. I vacationed there for the past four winters.

• I regularly write a travel column for ten suburban newspapers with a total circulation of 3 million.

• I regularly sell short stories to the *Paris Review, Esquire* and various university quarterlies.

Getting Assignments

Begin with a query. Query letters are sales letters. You sell yourself and your idea. In less than a page, you've gained an audition. Thanks to a few shiny paragraphs, an astute editor knows who you are and whether you have talent and know your subject.

The nuts and bolts of such letters are well explained in a mimeographed memo by the editors of *Moody Monthly:* Perhaps you're an old pro on queries. Relax. Do it your way. We do not hold out for a specific form or method, but we do need specifics. Be sure your approach includes:

1. *A working title* which will help us grab your idea quickly— not only the subject but slant or direction.
2. *A backup statement* suggesting why you think the proposed article would be appreciated by our kind of reader.
3. *Some indication of proposed treatment or approach*—anecdotal, reportorial, personal experience, message, etc. In some cases it may help to include main points as you foresee them.
4. *If you foresee problems* in handling a touchy subject, reassure us by telling us so and tell us how you intend to get around them.
5. *Don't forget mechanical details:* suggested length; availability of pictures; how soon you could do it.

On certain articles, it may be easier to take the précis route. This may include:

- An opening paragraph or two or three, followed by
- A listing of main points in sequence, and
- A wrapup statement of what the article would do for read-ers, treatment, proposed length, available pictures, etc.

Actually, most magazines will send you instructions like the above; you need only look up the address in the latest *Writers Market* and send the editors a self-addressed stamped envelope, known as a SASE.

Queries save the editor (and you) a lot of time. And once you have a good grip on your materials, you will find it easy to present your subject. Some specific examples:

Curtis W. Casewit
P.O. Box 19039
Denver, Colorado 80219
Phone (303) 935-0277

Query

Some of us travel so much that we develop a sixth sense about hotels. We may arrive in Calgary or Rome, Bom-bay or Mombasa, knowing we'll spend the night in a hotel that will soon show its personality, character, am-bience; it may even have its own "soul," as one French innkeeper once assured me. Before we register, we're already alert to the first impressions. What is the loca-tion like? The setting? How about the architecture? We get a glimpse of the facade; we seek clues about style and cleanliness from the windows and the glass doors. Cars and clientele indicate who comes here. Does the hotel aim to be different? We can tell something from the bellboys' uniforms; the doorman's face and the ex-tent of the welcome reveal the management's attitude.

This could be the lead of an article that might be titled, WHAT MAKES A GOOD HOTEL? It would be very much down my alley as a longtime travel writer, who has stayed in many of the world's best hotels.

I've kept a notebook of observations about the myriad things good hotels can do for the traveler. At the Grosvenor House in London, for instance, the staff actually goes out to buy you entire wardrobes or men's briefcases if necessary. My inspection notes include the Waldorf Astoria, plus hotels in Acapulco (mariachi band at a moment's notice), Baden-Baden, Zurich, Nice (doors fitted with red lights saying "Do not disturb"), San Francisco, West Berlin. I'm sure I could handle an anecdotal article assignment in 2,000 tight words.

You'll recognize my name from many magazines and from the covers of numerous books. Please drop me a line soon.

The query exudes enthusiasm; it sounds convincing. Obviously, the writer really visited all those hotels. The angle was promising, too!

* * * *

Query

It was my good fortune to recently travel for thirteen days with the English Chamber Orchestra, the Tashi Quartet, trumpet soloist Maurice André, soprano Jessye Norman (an American-born British national), Russian ballet dancers Galina and Valery Panov, and many others.

We were on a MUSIC CRUISE. A unique one: the performances alternately took place aboard our ship and ashore. The Panovs, for instance, danced on the floodlit decks while we docked at Pointe A Pitre, Guadelope. Miss Norman sang Purcell in an open country church on St. Croix. There was a musical gala al fresco on a banker's estate among the hillsides of Caracas. Pianists Pierre Barbizet, Arnaldo Cohen, Ruth Laredo played in the ship's grand salon while we were at sea.

(The vessel rolled so much one evening that the piano had to be tied down.)

I spoke with Peter Serkin, pianist son of Rudolph Serkin, about their lives. I interviewed Herr Mohr, the much-needed piano tuner aboard. I followed the *croisiere's* Hungarian impresario around. Some of the artists' names—Stoyka Nilanova, Aaron Rosand, Pinchas Zukerman—will be of interest to their fellow musicians on both sides of the Atlantic. In the past, Isaac Stern and Nureyev made the cruise, while the next one (August 31st to September 12th) will see Jean Pierre Rampal and Mstislav Rostropovich, among many others. (Locale: the Mediterranean.)

You'll agree that THE MUSIC CRUISE makes for an interesting concept. Do you see (as I do) an article possibility? Some of your readers may have been past passengers; others may plan to go but would like to know more details. Still others could simply find a vicarious pleasure in such an article.

Ideally, I'd like to write it in first person, present tense, diary fashion, with a touch of humor and even irreverence. It could be a compendium of stories, anecdotes, quotes, *bon mots.*

I'm a professional author (twenty published books) and contributor to numerous magazines. Anticipated thanks for your reaction and guidance regarding slant and wordage. I work on assignment.

The above shows what a travel article query should be like. It is a microcosm of the actual piece, complete with names and other details. It conveys an "I was there" feeling. Such a sales letter should be accompanied by some published sample stories, too, especially if the editor doesn't know your work.

Naturally, smaller and low-paying magazines don't expect you to go to all that trouble; if they pay you only $50 to $100 they just expect the manuscript. Let them have it; forget about the query.

Some travel writers are so well established and on such good terms with their magazine editors that they can propose an article in just a few lines. Here's an example:

" 'What Makes a Good Restaurant?' could describe some of my twenty years of coast-to-coast dining. I'd tell about many positive experiences at various restaurants and explain what makes a superior menu, cuisine, service, atmosphere.

"I would name some establishments in large cities, small towns, resorts, cite menus and write about mouthwatering meals. Here's a piece which could answer some people's statements that food isn't really important! Substitute title possibility: 'The Importance of Dining Well.' "

To be sure, it makes sense to look at the last few issues of your target publications to see if they've already run the article you are proposing. If so, it would mean automatic rejection for your idea. Incidentally, better magazines are indexed in the *Reader's Guide to Periodical Literature* which you find at your library.

Dealing with Magazine Editors

Keep in mind that your magazine contact has no obligation to accept your phone call unless you're known at the publication. And since editorial offices are deluged by offers, only the best ones elicit a response, and then only after weeks of waiting. (Some travel journalists actually knock on the magazine's door a second time after a month. Did Ms. X receive the query? Did Mr. Y have a chance to read it?)

Editors are most of all professionals; they're trained to take a dim view of misspellings, errors, or outdated materials—not to mention dull amateurish manuscripts. Few readers of your queries have the time to make comments, or to pat a good writer on the back. If they feel critical toward a piece of unsolicited writing, most editors would rather keep their opinions to themselves. They prefer to be diplomatic or noncommittal.

Exceptions exist, too. Not long ago, a professional article writer submitted a bushel of queries to a new editor, along with a number of published pieces as style samples.

To the writer's surprise, the package was returned with the following caustic comment: "Your latest writing samples have served only to confirm my unwillingness to assign work to you. Your writing is, to my eye and ear, utterly undistinguished. Your leads are lifeless and dull. The stories resemble the leads."

While some writers deserve contempt for their sloppiness and lack of professionalism, a few magazine editors are no angels, either: they give assignments to several writers and pick the best; they may toss proposals into the wastebasket, refuse to return phone calls to pros who worked for the magazine before, or neglect to put through a voucher for an accepted article. (The writer may have to wait three months for his money.) On the other hand, many amateurs irritate editors by refusing to study the publication; these careless researchers fail to tell apart the difference between one magazine's scholarly tone and a competitor's, which may use a less serious and more popular style.

Editors should therefore be forgiven for not wanting to deal with the lazy, the inept or the stupid. In general, if you work with a good magazine, an assignment implies serious consideration; in case of a rejection you will be paid at least a portion of the promised article fee. This is called a *kill fee* or *salvage fee*.

Travel Article Buyers

Now that you know what a query should look like and have actually typed it neatly on your obligatory letterhead, you will need to figure out where to send it.

Which magazines buy travel articles? Who considers newcomers? Where do you have a chance?

The answers to these questions will mean the difference between success and failure in the writing business. Indeed, by now your emphasis should be completely on marketing. This takes initiative, resourcefulness and most of all, persistence.

You can get the easiest foothold at the nearest city magazine. Almost every major American (or Canadian) city has its own publication aimed at the local folks. Some examples:

Denver Magazine
Philadelphia Magazine
Los Angeles Magazine
Metro Phoenix Magazine
Cleveland Magazine
San Francisco Magazine
Palm Springs Life

to name just a few.

In addition, you will find women's regional magazines like *Boston Woman, New York Woman, San Diego Woman* and many more.

What are the advantages of these city publications? First of all, most use some regional travel; the pages are aimed at newcomers or residents and often meant to back up local ads. Second, the editors don't like to offend local readers like yourself who may be subscribers as well. In general, the doors are therefore open to your suggestions. And third, unless you're a New Yorker who wants to write for the elistist *New York* magazine, you can generally approach editors by phone. They will even return your calls.

It is true that some of these city publications may have their own travel writer (just check the masthead). But more often than not, the magazines will publish a few special travel issues to which you might be able to contribute. Naturally, it takes some crass opportunism and ingeniousness to come up with the best possible idea. As always, the better the pay, the more competition.

State, provincial and regional magazines go somewhat farther afield; the whole state or province is their oyster. Among many others you might consider, are

California Magazine (prestigious, sophisticated, well-paying)
New Mexico Magazine
Arizona Monthly
Yankee
Ohio Magazine
Texas Monthly (literary, intelligent)

The list could be extended through the rest of the United States and Canada; keep in mind that each publication has its own editorial policies, philosophies and remuneration. (The addresses of the publication will be found in your yearly *Writer's Market*.)

General and Consumer Magazines

To be sure, most North American publications find space for an occasional travel article; in some cases, regularly. It just takes a trip to the nearest university library, or the largest public library in your area, to convince you that opportunity exists aplenty for the travel scribe. Check your news dealers, too; a little browsing will show you that the most common publications on the stands—*Better Homes & Gardens, Modern Bride, Cosmopolitan, Gentlemen's Quarterly, Esquire* and dozens more—use freelance travel stories. The elegant women's magazines such as *Vogue, Harper's Bazaar, Glamour* may be hard to hit but they all buy travel, as do such slick "books" as *Vanity Fair, Architectural Digest, Town & Country.*

At the same time, fraternal male-oriented publications of the Lions Club, the Kiwanis and others are possible markets, along with the outdoor "slicks" for fishing and hunting locales. Each group of publications has its own travel axes to grind. Thus, a health magazine may be interested in a new or especially effective spa, a new clinic or other health-related travel topic. The assorted AAA magazines may not only go for destinations but also articles on how to drive your car there in foul weather, ice and snow. Numer-

ous senior publications—*Modern Maturity* comes to mind—
buy travel for their retired readers; in fact, there are all
kinds of regional senior publications as well. (Some of
them, like *New England Senior Citizen,* pay modestly but are
courteous to writers.) Military magazines (*Off Duty, R & R*)
are often located overseas and therefore a little more difficult to deal with; however, if you get to their offices in the
Frankfurt area or Hong Kong, these magazines become via-
ble markets. Naturally, you could opt to freelance for a professional travel agent's monthly such as *Asta Agency
Management,* the *Travel Agent* and others. In this case, you are
expected to know something about the agency business.

Travel and In-flight Magazines

Where are the biggest possibilities?

To be sure, the huge field of travel magazines deserves
study for its diversity, with almost every editor addressing a
different customer, or audience. The demographics vary as
much as the educational and income levels of the *Travel &
Leisure, Travel/Holiday, Ford Times, Condé Nast Traveler, National Geographic, Westways* or *Diversion* reader. A page-by-
page scrutiny of each magazine, complete with a study of
advertising, will give you a clue to subjects, treatment and
language. (*Diversion,* for instance, is edited for doctors.)

The "in-flight" publications have merged and changed
names and even publishers during the past decade. But almost every airline has one of these magazines, which are
read by traveling executives who are interested in travel.
Some of the firms that have become rich on ads for hotels,
rental cars, resorts, condos and computers now operate as
many as a dozen of these give-away monthlies. They represent a fabulous market for the travel writer with an eye on
the current, the topical, the interesting. Read the in-flight
magazine you are interested in to see if it publishes travel
articles; some do business or celebrity profiles only. Payment ranges all the way from a free airline ticket from Denver to Aspen to $100 and even $1,000. As always, the better

paying editors get their pick of articles, and are therefore difficult to sell to because of competition and high standards.

The Religious Field

Would you believe that even a Catholic, Protestant or Jewish magazine buys travel articles? The answer is yes, and for good reason: religious readers voyage to the Holy Land, or set out to see churches, cathedrals, synagogues, the cemeteries or monuments of their destinations.

Success can be immediate. Among others, I know:

• A lady who persuaded a regional Christian magazine to let her describe a different church every month. Her husband, a minister who was nimble with the drawing pen, illustrated each article.

• An alert seventeen-year-old who parlayed a summer at an Israeli kibbutz into a very readable article; it found an immediate home in a Zionist magazine.

• A novice writer who, while in Switzerland, was introduced to the late but fascinating Catholic philosopher and lecturer, mountain climber and skier, Sir Arnold Lunn. Result: a first article which sold for good money to *Catholic Digest.*

The list could go on and on.

You should be able to place travel-related material in due time to many religious magazines.

Making Multiple Sales and Cashing In on Spin-offs

A travel writer can't live by one article sale alone; the professional thinks in multiples. We have already seen that only a few newspapers expect an exclusive from you. A story can therefore appear simultaneously in Boston and Denver, Toronto and Dallas, or wherever.

The magazine field is a little more complicated. First of

all, the days of the nineteen fifties and sixties are long gone; during those decades, you could not even offer a query to two editors at the same time.

Now, with the blessings of the various writers' organizations, professional travel writers send out simultaneous queries. For a James Michener and his agent, this procedure is nothing new; a famous writer calls his own shots in the market place. Likewise, the top "name" travel writers are sufficiently in demand to offer their latest China reports to the highest bidder among the magazines.

How about the mass of professionals? Most of them know that editors are so swamped with offers that two magazines are unlikely to commission the same piece; if this were to happen, the ethical travel journalist quickly informs one of them that the market choice has been made.

Ideas for travel features, especially topical and fashionable ones, are perishable; multiple queries therefore assure a speedy decision. The method simply assures a writer's survival. To be sure, magazines have their own slants, so the same idea, even if accepted, would have to be written differently for a competing publication.

To make money, the *journaliste de voyages* thinks in terms of spin-offs. What's that? An example: A few years ago, I was invited by their respective governments to see Kenya and Zambia. The trip took two and a half weeks. Money had to be made. I therefore decided to conceive several articles from my long visit. The first and major piece had to do with photo safaris in Africa, which was then a new idea. It included walking tours, nuts and bolts service data on hotels, costs and so on. This article was done for a travel publication.

While being surrounded by wild elephants, zebras, reeboks and other creatures, it also occurred to me that a short piece on African animals would sell to a children's magazine. No sooner thought than done; I'd concentrate on these manuscipts at night in longhand before bedtime. Finally, after several weeks of travel, I became aware of the whites' plight: they were being driven out by the Zambian blacks. Many of these white settlers were English, yet they'd never been to England; they'd been brought up in Africa and felt African. Where would their children go to school? Would it be permissible to take their cars along to Europe? And how about their savings? The conversations had an impact on me, and I wound up with a third spin-off from the trip—a political story about the whites in Zambia, which I sold to a well-paying fraternal publication. Two and a half weeks. Three articles.

Likewise, one can spend seven days on a cruise ship where an industrious travel writer could cook up numerous stories. First of all, there is the theme cruise itself. One typical voyage deals with the understanding of certain Canadian provinces which include Quebec, New Brunswick and Prince Edward Island. The ports-of-call are worth writing about, too. The lecturer aboard helps you with a historical focus.

At the same time, you notice that the Mediterranean dishes on the Greek ship are delicious, so you write a second travel article, this one dealing with the food.

The purser introduces you to the Greek captain, and at dinner, as you listen to this man and his devotion to the sea, you realize that a profile of the captain would make an interesting article. Spin-offs from *one* cruise!

A Word About Rights

The wise novice travel writer invests much time to learn the craft and get proficient in marketing. A complete law study should be left to the lawyers or to the magazines themselves. Nevertheless, some rudimentary terms must be explained.

A few newcomers actually write a copyright sign © on page one of every manuscript. This is unnecessary for novices. Since 1976, every magazine article enjoys automatic copyright, just like a photograph or a painting. You are protected as long as you live, plus fifty years. Some professional travel journalists go a step further: they register each article with the Copyright Office in Washington, D.C. This takes time and money, of course. Why do they do it? Such a registration allows them to sue anyone who infringes on their copyright. The new writer needn't worry about such legal niceties.

The same situation applies to the famous "work for hire" provision. Travel guide book publishers and certain magazines make you sign such a clause. It means that you were hired to write a piece and that *they* own it. Writers' organizations vociferously object. The new scribe hasn't much of a leg to stand on; to make money, one must sign such agreements. I gladly do. After all, the guide book publisher had the good sense to employ me to produce certain material. And I get paid.

Writers also often place the words "First North American Serial Rights" on top of their manuscripts. It means that they grant a magazine the right to publish an article first but just once; the publisher doesn't own the copyright. The latter remains with the author. This, too, seems unnecessary, and may be detrimental to the apprentice travel journalist. In fact, I know of some editors who have rejected a manuscript because of the author's legal warnings. (Naturally, after some years of successful publishing, authors may want to read a good book on the subject; see index.)

Lastly, some magazines rubber stamp "all rights" or "world rights" on the backs of their checks. What should you do about it? Some of my colleagues suggest that you send it back to the publisher for re-issue. I disagree. You may never see any other check. Other writers cross off the offensive "world rights" and then cash the check. Such action, however, could result in a transaction that the bank will not honor.

Naturally, it all depends. A well-known Boston newspaper once sent a $50 payment, with the "world rights" proviso, to a travel specialist of my acquaintance. My *confrère* cashed it quickly, then proceeded to sell the same piece to other newspapers. On the other hand, $500 or more should pacify any writer to sign and give an exclusive.

A Word About Money

The travel writer has little say about money. You don't tell the editor how much you want to charge for a magazine piece. Instead, you will be told what the magazine can offer. You can take it or leave it. This applies to the average mortal; a James Michener, Paul Theroux or John Updike is in another league; they'll be asked.

Fees vary.

Some religious publications pay as little as twenty dollars for a short feature. A $50 check is common with low-circulation consumer, family, travel trade, or senior magazines.

Feeder airlines, minor health publications, regional Sunday supplements buy travel at about $100. The rates have barely gone up since the early nineteen seventies.

A large number of "slick" monthlies (the slick has to do with paper quality) will pay several hundred dollars.

Lastly, there are certain mass market magazines—for home makers, for contemporary women, for fashion-conscious males—who will part with $800 to four-figure checks; the group also includes *Travel & Leisure*, *Reader's Digest* and a few others, all equally hard to hit.

The promise of payment doesn't automatically or reliably put dollars into your bank account. A check on acceptance is rare these days when business in the United States is done on a "pay after thirty or sixty days."

One in a hundred magazines goes out of business before the accountants can pay you. One in a hundred may delay check-writing for six months; some only react to a

letter from your lawyer or to a collection agency.
The smart travel writer doesn't lose any sleep over this.
Tant pis. The trip itself was lovely.

9

Selling Travel Books

Opportunity in Travel Guides

Here's a somewhat startling piece of information.

It is reasonably easy to sell a book on travel even if you are an unpublished newcomer. Even if you are completely unknown. This is, as we have seen, the opposite of the newspaper and magazine markets.

Sound unusual? Indeed, it can sometimes be easier to place a travel guide than to hit the *Chicago Tribune* or the *Christian Science Monitor* with an article.

Keep in mind that publishing a book involves some prestige. A book is more permanent than newspapers. A newspaper article, despite the joy of creating it, is perishable. But a book, even a paperback, gets on library shelves, possibly brings royalties to you and your children and in some cases even to your grandchildren.

My book *Freelance Writing,* for instance, was written in 1973 and has brought me a royalty check twice a year ever since.

Basically the chief premise of selling a travel book is originality. Indeed, the editor immediately will want to know: Is your idea fresh? Is it new? Has it ever been done before? Is it something the public needs?

Here's one good example.

Some years ago, Lois Weiss conceived a travel guide for the handicapped. No such text existed then; she understood the needs of people in wheel chairs and readers with various afflictions who also wanted to get around the world. She wrote a manuscript which dealt with airline rules, bus ramps, railroads, and so forth.

Lois Weiss immediately sold her idea. In fact, the paperback saw several editions and while there are now some competing titles, this one is the best in its field.

The updating calls for a lot of travel on her part and the periodic revisions keep her busy. Financially, one might assume the various editions of the text grossed her $20,000 to $25,000. The travel is satisfying and Lois Weiss derives a special joy from helping others. She had not done much writing before she created *Access to the World: A Guide for the Handicapped.*

It was the novelty of her idea which brought her publication.

An acquaintance of mine was successful in putting together an inexpensive little paperback which you can find in bookstores, entitled *The New Guide—Where You Can Vacation in America on $5 a Day.* And he subtitles it, *The Guide to Low Cost Vacations and Lodgings on College Campuses.* Namely, he discovered that on any college in summer, when classes aren't in session, you can rent a student room for about $3–$8. Conditions may be very spartan. I've tried it. But you can play tennis and you can have a grand time, and save a lot of money. Now this was a new idea, something anyone out there could have done. It doesn't require great writing ability.

Many new titles are written by novices in the business. A former travel journalism student who loves to fish persuaded Rand McNally to accept a manuscript which he called *Fishing Hot Spots*. It's a practical guide on where to fish around the United States. There are many books on the technique of fishing and the equipment you need, but not many on where to do it.

John Wiley & Sons recently brought out R. Axtell's *The Dos and Taboos Around the World—A Guide to International Behavior*. The author is obviously someone who travels. Perhaps he/she is an executive recruiter, perhaps a State Department person, a foreign service officer, someone retired from the Air Force.

On occasion religion can lend itself to a guide.

The Jewish Traveler is a well-advertised Doubleday title. It covers fifty-two cities. The writer was very busy going to the various temples and synagogues and holy places, even to restaurants serving kosher food.

You could probably do a guide for the Moslems of the United States or for the Presbyterians, and so on.

I know a woman who lives on Cape Cod whose husband is a minister. The two of them decided to collaborate on a religious travel guide. She is a competent writer. And so they did *The Churches of New England*. This was a natural for her. At the time nothing else was published regionally quite like it.

The idea needs to fit you like a glove, of course. You need to be comfortable with it.

Originality

If you propose another book on Hawaii it needs to be something totally different from all the current Hawaii guides. Which means extra research. This includes visiting book stores, assuring yourself that such a title, *your* title, doesn't exist as yet. That you have no competition.

A recent *Publisher's Weekly* carried an ad for *How to Beat the High Cost of Travel*, a book which renders a service to the reader. It's a paperback that could become popular because many people want to travel on a budget.

If you visit New York City be sure to go to the Traveller's Bookstore in Manhattan; it stocks every travel guide in the business. And you can go to your own local bookstore. Head for the travel section and take a look at what is being published.

Examples?

• On a recent bookseller foray, I found such unique titles as these:

• *The Spa Book.* Two writers toured all the major spas in Europe, from Montecatini to Baden-Baden, from Bucharest to Vichy. In the United States they visited the "beauty farms". They went to the Canyon Ranch. What an original approach!

• *Travel and the Single Woman.* How to beat off the males who always want to dine with her. How to discourage the bellboys to linger. Again, an excellent idea with the solo female travel slant.

• *The Discount Guide for Travellers Over 55.* Another narrow area where an older author found a niche for himself.

• *The World Guide to Nude Beaches.* A unique concept which the publisher can offer in many countries.

• *Haunted Houses.* Here's a collection of 30 haunted houses from coast to coast, with photos and all. A different approach to travel guides!

• *Ferries of America.* Sarah Bird Wright, a travel writing student of mine, came upon this unique idea while on a trip. She almost immediately found a publisher for her concept, a review of America's many ferries.

• *Caribbean Ports of Call.* Sure, there exist some guides to the various Caribbean islands, but none specifically for the *cruise ship passenger*.

• *Europe by Eurail.* Most people are familiar with the Eurailpass, which is a ticket good for most European countries. Now someone did a book just for the rail fan. Interesting.

• *Europe's Hidden Flea Markets?* Great idea.

- *Europe's Wonderful Little Hotels.* Good.
- *The Paradores of Spain.* An excellent approach.
- *Turn Left at the Pub.* This is a longtime paperback about sightseeing in various European cities. "Where the Antiques are in Britain." Wonderful.

All these titles owe their existence to the fact that they're *unique.*

To be sure, apprentice travel guide writers are often afraid of authoring a book manuscript. A book! How could they possibly find the stamina to research, organize and finally write 200–300 manuscript pages, even if they could think of an original idea?

That depends. If you know your subject, the task isn't as daunting as you might think.

Some magazine writers, after switching to books, admit that ten or twelve chapters correspond more or less with ten to twelve magazine articles. And some short nonfiction writers put together as many as forty magazine articles a year.

Naturally, a book achieves more depth and contains more detail than a magazine piece. Writing it will take a little more digging, a little more accuracy-checking. As you embark on the job, you will find that practice brings speed, it gets easier because you become more familiar with the material as you get into it. And you can put together the book pages fairly fast.

How to Get Ideas

How do you come up with original ideas? One of the very first titles I ever sold, *How to Get a Job Overseas*, was the result of being a book buyer at a large department store. I asked the clerk what type of international paperback they had calls for but which was unavailable from the publishers. (To know if a book exists, ask to see the *Subject Guide* of *Bowkers Books in Print*.) I was told that everyday someone asked for a paperback on how to get a job overseas. Those were the good years when Americans all wanted to be abroad. In the recent (terrorism) years my book has slowed down, but it had about a ten-year-life. I knew the title was needed because retailers had requests for it. (Moral of story: Make friends with your bookseller.)

I had never written a book at that time. I boldly approached a publisher, saying that a certain large, famous department store had calls for *How to Get a Job Overseas*. May I propose such a title and write it? Whereupon they said okay, "Give us a sample chapter." So all it took were twenty pages or so and a sale was made. In fact, I shortly quit my job as a book buyer and set out to Europe and the rest of the world to do research.

An enterprising, ambitious novice could contact the local book wholesaler and some of the managers at the big chain stores like Waldenbooks and B. Dalton and pose the same questions I did several decades ago. What type of travel guides are presently nonexistent? What does the public ask for but can't get? If the manager were a travel writer, what type of project would he/she propose to a publisher?

Certainly, a frequent study of *Publisher's Weekly* magazine will yield some clues. Study the publisher's ads for related ideas. (And if you *do* have an idea, you can find out if another writer has beat you to the punch recently.)

Here's an example. Let's say, you are fully aware of the popularity of bed & breakfast guides. You'd like to do one, too. If you are a hard-working travel journalist, you will check the *Publisher's Weekly* listings and ads for such titles, as well as *Books in Print*. Suppose there is no listing about boarding houses, historic hotels or B&B's in the Rocky Mountain region. Solution? Offer a guide to a publisher! Before long, you could have a contract for *Country Inns of the Rocky Mountain Region*. It's your first book. (I hasten to say this has been done.)

Good concepts emerge from the times: as this is written the dollar buys less and less in Japan and Europe. As a result, true budget guides will interest the economy traveler and thus your editor.

The resourceful newcomer could probably sell a book on ashrams, kibbutzim, Club Meds, biking trails. Actually, the list is endless, merely depending on your interests.

Becoming a Regional Editor for an Established Travel Guide

Another way of getting a good idea and selling a travel guide (one which you can market immediately), is to return to the first-class bookstore, visit the travel sections and study very, very carefully the established *series* guides. Did Fodor or Frommer or Fielding and a host of other editors already publish a certain title which you have in mind? Is there something these longtime travel specialists have left out, some small area that they have forgotten? Do you have a new angle? You write Mr. Birnbaum and you say, "Have you ever considered doing a title on such and such? Couldn't find the writer? Let me do it for you." And you might get a contract for the job.

Best of all, you can also apply to major guide book publishers as a "regional" editor, i.e., you will be responsible to update the regional Birnbaum or Frommer titles. It isn't difficult to get these (part-time) local jobs; you merely need some published writing samples. In one case, a woman actually held the PR position for a local museum; in another, an old-time restaurateur of a certain city applied and was "hired" for a "job" which actually takes only a few weeks or two months per year. Naturally, you need to prove that you know your city extremely well, that you have the kind of local contacts which will guarantee the accuracy of your guide revisions or additions.

If you study a typical travel guide series, say, the volumes put out by the American Automobile Association, you will quickly become aware of the editors' approach. No literary pretense. A straightforward style. Basic information, simply and intelligently presented.

Unlike the literary travel literature, most guides stick to a format; while this is different for Frommer, Fodor's, Fisher's, Harvard's Let's Go and many others, the writer is kept within bounds. Hotels, restaurants, museums, shopping, local entertainment, sightseeing are all presented in plain prose; indeed, most of the guide book writers (also known as regional editors) aim for the practical; few of these people have any dreams to be another Paul Theroux or Kate Simon or Peter Mathiessen.

True: the regional editors know their area, or the region (country, province) into which they're sent; they report mostly facts to their readers in bread and butter language; in fact, they'd get nervous if they were asked to write elegantly or eruditely à la *New Yorker*.

In short, you don't have to be a British stylist or a famous poet to be asked to do the Omaha, Nebraska, section of Frommer's midwestern guide.

You only have to be industrious enough to obtain all the local facts and put them together in such a fashion that any reader gets the information. Indeed, once you knock on the publisher's door and are asked to come in on an area basis, you will receive editorial instructions on how to proceed. Nothing is left to your imagination. And no "top of the head" writing, either.

The Nuts and Bolts Guide Versus the Literary Book

Luckily, a few (very few!) people have the keen sense of observation and talent to bring some color to their assigned book chapters. Such literary types naturally appeal to armchair travelers, who often buy the authors' product.

Good writing isn't especially rewarding financially; all guide book contributors and "revisors" (the same people who also revise old guides) receive the same sums. Each publisher has its own formula for payment which is modest. (Expenses? Few publishers reimburse you but travel costs make permissible tax deductions.) The checks are generally reliable, often on a work for hire basis (you own no rights and get no future profits). Only in a few cases, writers are asked to contribute, promised a certain small sum and then not paid. In short, the guide book industry is generally free of fly-by-nights or deadbeats.

To be sure, the Frommers, Fieldings, *Insight* guides, *Access Guides* and many others make up only the commercial part of the field. The majority of book publishers will also consider the more literary offerings: First-person adventures in faraway countries, usually by someone who is known as an explorer; specialized, scholarly observations about a country's art and architecture (again requiring credentials); accounts of trips by famous authors (such as Steinbeck's classic *Travels with Charley*) or a literary mix.

Quite often the authors are novelists who do travel books only occasionally; among others, you might study Mary McCarthy, Lawrence Durrell, Eric Newby, Graham Greene.

The book author with literary aspirations will satisfy personal creative urges. But for the unknown, publication is not guaranteed. In fact, it may be a long struggle. Practical guides are easier to place. More about this shortly.

All About Book Proposals and How to Sell Them

You begin a book sale with still another trip to your favorite large bookshop or to a sizable up-to-date city library. Ask for the travel section. Now which publisher puts out titles like those you have in mind? The names of the publishers appear on the spine of the books and inside. Make a note of who does what, then concentrate on the *Literary Market Place* for the names of editors. (The LMP is available at your library.)

Most travel book offers start with the query. It is the same type of letter already discussed for article writers.

Basically you need to say who you are, why a publisher should trust you, why the material is close to your heart, what kind of knowledge you have that enables you to undertake the project. In your letter you ask if the publisher wants to see a *prospectus*.

A prospectus is a six to ten page outline for your book. Before you even write a letter you prepare such a proposal and have it ready for the publisher. In the prospectus you

list the entire market scene, i.e., who else is currently offering your type of project. Such a market study isn't difficult
to do for a newcomer. You spend a day at a good bookstore;
you look at what other titles are available; and you look
through R. R. Bowker's *Forthcoming Books*. You also need to
tell the editor why your project will be successful, how many
copies you hope to sell. Should it be in hardback or in
paperback? These decisions will be ultimately made by the
publisher but he would appreciate your input up front.

The important thing is to put yourself into the publisher's shoes. If you were this person, what would you want
to know about a concept? You'd be eager to know about
sales: to whom can the book be sold, what kind of audience
you have in mind, and why the readers would buy your title
instead of someone else's.

A few of these details can already appear in your first
letter. One that whets an editor's appetite:

Query (nonfiction)

Strange situation: Through the years America has been
plagued by inflation, recessions, unemployment and a
recent stock market crash. Yet the U.S. ski industry
thrives: according to trade magazines and airlines,
there're now some six million American skiers who
spend nearly four billion dollars each winter for equipment, travel, lodging and other ski-related items.

Strange situation, which prompts this professional
writer's questions: Why do so few publishers cash in on
this affluent market, especially on ski *travel?* Why are
there so few North American ski guides?

More: *Why has no one zeroed in on the U.S.' leading ski
state, namely Colorado?*

That's why I'd like to propose an inexpensive travel
guide, to be written for skiers (of all kinds) by a skier
and long-time Colorado resident. My book would have
one chapter each about the state's leading resorts, complete with info on slopes, hostelries, atmosphere and
general characteristics. Because nearly all skiers come

to Denver, I'd include a chapter on the capital. The book need not list prices; the writing would be lively and yet general enough to reduce updating. (A revised edition would only come out every five years.)

You may remember my name as the author of numerous ski books, an airline travel guide to Colorado, a lavish, bestselling coffee-table book on the state and countless articles in the regional ski doings. I'm the former editor of *Leisure Living Magazine*, a fanatic (though average) skier, and the author of the *Popular Library* paperback titled *The Compleat Skier*. The book concentrates on general ski travel, equipment, technique, and the European ski resorts.

My working title: THE SKIER'S GUIDE TO COLORADO.

May I send you a detailed prospectus? If it were acceptable, what sort of advance could you pay?

Such a letter should be typed on your stationery; the presentation must be flawless and 100% accurate. Check your bookstore for leads regarding publishers, and look up the editors' names in the *Literary Market Place*, available at a library.

The query can be sent to the most likely publishers at the same time; editors expect most authors to query simultaneously, though many do not. (If you didn't, you go bankrupt; no pro can wait three months for an answer until trying another publisher.)

The important thing about the letter: a good idea showing your enthusiasm for your subject gets your foot into the door.

That's why you must immediately offer more, for example: "May I send you a prospectus?"

Your first sales attempt must not waste the editor's time; be direct and tell clearly what you have to offer. Write tightly.

Prospectus (nonfiction)

Thanks for your interest in a paperback titled

FOREIGN JOBS: THE BEST COUNTRIES

There should be a large market for an inexpensive book on jobs abroad. A local pocketbook rep and a librarian told me that there is currently no other up-to-date paperback, nor library edition, on the above topic. And Bowker's confirms it!

I travel far and wide on business and pleasure; during the past twelve months, for instance, I flew to Europe five times. I've personally interviewed many executive recruiters, state labor authorities, *Arbeitsaemter* and overseas Americans in many countries on the Continent. The paperback would focus on the possibilities in Scandinavia, Germany, Switzerland; in addition, I'd write about the employment situation in New Zealand, Australia and Israel as well.

After a detailed outline of the chapters and other important material I concluded my presentation like this:

I'm a much-published travel columnist (thirty newspapers), contributor to many travel magazines and author of eight travel guides. I work with major airlines and international tourist organizations and speak four languages fluently. I authored twenty nonfiction titles that include *Seasonal Jobs on Land and Sea, Inside Overseas Jobs, Strategies to Get the Job You Want,* and the bestselling paperback, *Freelance Writing: Advice From the Pros* which has sold 150,000 copies and was followed last year by a book for painters and sculptors dealing with the commercial nitty-gritty and nuts and bolts of their profession, *Making a Living in the Fine Arts.*

Apart from a membership in the Travel Journalist Guild, I'm a member of the Federation Internationale Des Journalistes Et Ecrivains Du Tourisme (World Federation of Travel Writers and Journalists).

What to do if you can't cite such credits? If that's the case, ask yourself how you came to the travel book idea and why you want to pursue it. Tell the editor or publisher. Your enthusiasm may catch.

Magazine or newspaper credits are often less impor-tant than a new author's eagerness. Illustration? One Uni-versity of Colorado student had no writing experience or published prior books. But he'd just spent two uninter-rupted years on the island of Crete. He'd personally hiked, cycled, boated and slept in every part of the island. He'd made copious notes. He had no publication credits but he appeared enthusiastic.

In another case, a student had sold numerous newspa-per articles about small hotels in the west which led to a request for a prospectus and a book contract.

The ideal prospectus should also contain a carefully thought-out and presented contents page for your project. This requires an overall view and genuine knowledge in your subject area.

Your chapters must be outlined in great detail.

Here is an example from my overseas jobs paperback. Note the progression within the chapter:

Chapter IV.

A JOB ABROAD: HOW TO GO ABOUT IT. How to start investigating possibilities while still in the U.S. How to research the situation through U.S. government offices, colleges, travel agencies, tourist offices, banks, return-ees. Making your way overseas via a U.S. firm. How to break into the job market. Researching, writing letters. A close look at employment agencies and recruiters and how they operate. Getting interviewed. Your chances with foreign firms. Getting data about visas, work per-mits and residence permits. Useful addresses of Ameri-can firms and colleges.

Individual publishers have their own concept of what makes the ideal prospectus or outline. Even small houses tell their would-be authors what they expect. One small press in New England sends the following instructions to prospective authors:

- Please submit a two-to-four page typed outline, indicating the nature and scope of each chapter, as well as significant appendices. Also tell us:
- Your proposed title
- Anticipated manuscript length
- Titles of any previously published books or articles
- Briefly (about 50 words) why you think your treatment of the subject will be unique (unavailable in other books)
- Briefly (about 50 words) where/how you intend to collect and verify the factual information you'll be including
- Briefly (about 50 words) why you are particularly qualified to write on this subject

Working with a Book Publisher

Many years ago, when the book business was more casual and publishing accountants not all-powerful, the pro could sell a nonfiction book on the basis of a good outline and a few published magazine articles to indicate style.

Today, almost every publisher demands one or more sample chapters as well. This is tough on the author; providing a twenty-five-page sample is almost as involving and time-consuming as doing the entire manuscript. And there seem to be few exceptions to the rule, at least not for someone whose name is not a household word. Thus an experienced colleague received a letter from his literary agent which spelled out the situation.

> I think what X, or any other publisher who may yet express interest, would like to see is about two sample chapters per book; which is not an unusual request even when authors with your excellent track record are involved—it's the book they're primarily worried about, not you.

Simon & Schuster's general reference division even goes to the trouble to tell prospective authors just what's needed:

"Select one or two chapters of the manuscript which are an integral part of the book. They should be the best written chapters; they need not be sequential. For example, you might submit Chapters 3 and 14 of a twenty-chapter book, as long as these chapters best reflect the book's content and your writing style. It is also advisable to submit any chapter that is particularly innovative or unique.

"Sample chapters should contain rough sketches, charts, handwritten equations and descriptions of photographs to be included. The purpose is simply to give the reviewers and publisher an idea of the format of the book; the material need not be in final form. In preparing the chapters, the primary emphasis should be on readability."

Of course, to the beginner, sample chapters are a must. You have to prove yourself, to show how you write. Think of it this way: A partial manuscript is good practice for you. In short, the investment of time is well worth your while. If you do a good job, you will get a contract for the book.

There is never a guarantee, however. The editor may have seen a just-published title like yours, one you didn't know about. The editor may have liked the idea but he was shot down by his colleagues at the weekly conference. Maybe your editor got fired, or changed publishers, before he could present your prospectus to the powers-that-be.

Take heart. For many years, the story made the rounds in publishing circles that someone turned down *Kon Tiki*, one of the greatest travel adventures of all time. The editor wrote, "Who in hell wants to read about a bunch of crazy Scandinavians on a raft?" The rest of the story applies to you, too: *Kon Tiki*, like many other first-rejected books, became a bestseller.

Many newcomers have received contracts for a travel book because of a first-rate idea, a convincing letter and that outstanding prospectus.

Once you have the contract the publisher will give you a deadline. It varies from house to house and project, usually eight months to a year. You may receive an advance against royalties. How much? You get anywhere from $1,000 to $10,000, $15,000, part of it upon signing the contract, part of it upon delivery of the manuscript. Then you sally forth and write the book. (Not all publishers pay advances. You will need to inquire about this. Royalty levels are nego-tiable and should be discussed also.)

Naturally, the success of your project will have a lot to do with the good luck of being assigned a good editor. The best of the breed are creative, gentle, unobtrusive; they make pencilled suggestions that a writer may or may not accept. They praise and guide, working from a thorough knowledge of the marketplace. The ideal travel book editor doesn't rewrite; that's up to the author. Nor does the editor force personal opinions on you. (The latter should be so brilliant that the author can't resist them.) "I've met editors I'd follow into the sea," says one longtime writer.

Personally, I've worked with perhaps twenty to thirty editors, some at very large publishing firms. I found that the ideal ones go to bat on behalf of the author's book; they manage to enthuse their colleagues and later twist the arm of the ad manager for more promotion; in short, they help make a travel book a success.

The Lucrative "Premium" Market and Other Book Promotion

Are you someone with good connections? Someone who knows a travel-related executive with clout? An airline vice president? The top guns at travel clubs, railroads, hotel chains? An influential national tourist office honcho?

If so, you may be able to make a "premium book" sale even before you have a publisher. To explain: some years ago, I was introduced to an all-powerful airline executive. As we chatted, I asked him if he'd ever thought of a paper-back as a vehicle to promote the carrier? A paperback, say about western ski resorts, which could be sold at cost in the airline ads; such a book could also be sent to important travel agency customers to remind them of the airline. And finally, it could be sold by a publisher to the general public at book stores. A written proposal later, we began to discuss the idea in earnest. Within six weeks, I had an okay from the airline which would pay me $8,000 plus expenses. The arrangement pleased a major publisher, too, which printed our guide some eight months later, just in time for the winter season.

Premium books only depend on your aggressiveness and opportunism. After writing some newspaper travel pieces about a certain state's many ski areas, I approached the ski area association. How about a book? I'd find the publisher for it if the association could guarantee purchase of 10,000 copies and pay me $3,000 for the expenses to research and write the guide. The association agreed; eventually, a publisher was willing to advance me $5,000 for the project and we were underway.

A large national tourist office, a major travel club, a group of travel agencies, a bed & breakfast association, airlines, cruise lines may all be in the market for books. It merely depends on your initiative to find out. The large publishers like Doubleday, Simon & Schuster, Random House and many more, all have special premium sales managers who will be eager to work with you. There are even some specialized New York-based companies which only do premium books. Naturally, when guaranteed sales are available even the smallest press will be willing to listen.

Ideally, the travel guide author should be promotion-minded. The author cannot count 100% on the publisher's sales department; instead, the author shows sample copies to anyone who will listen. Keep in mind that the more copies the publisher sells, the better your royalties, which are generally paid every six months.

I gladly make the rounds of retail book stores, shaking hands, sweet-talking buyers (no high pressure, please), calling on wholesalers, distributors, going on radio in various cities (all self-arranged), offering interviews to television stations, tipping off reporters about the book (and getting publicity out of that) and so on. I know much about my book's subject and am its most enthusiastic promoter.

Such promotion can cost you money, of course. I once flew to the Frankfurt International Book Fair at my own expense; while there I helped the (small) publisher in his booth, greeting retailers from all over the world.

Michael Sedge, author of several international travel guides, recently told his colleagues of a large writers' group how he felt about it all.

"Even if you do not like the idea of promoting, keep in mind that while you are pushing your books, you are also promoting yourself as a writer. I have been invited to speak at several gatherings and appear on television and radio, and have had a number of articles written about me as an author, due to my promotional efforts. Most of this led to more work—and money. It could for you, too."

Appendix:
Major PR Contacts
in the United States

Alabama Bureau of Tourism and Travel, 532 South Perry Street, Montgomery, Alabama 36704.

Alaska Division of Tourism, Pouch E, Juneau, Alaska 99811.

Arizona Office of Tourism, 1480 East Bethany Home Road, Suite 180, Phoenix, Arizona 85014.

California Office of Tourism, 1121 L Street, First Floor, Sacramento, California 95814.

Colorado Ski Country USA, 1560 Broadway, Denver, Colorado 80202.

Connecticut Department of Economic Development, Tourism, 210 Washington Street, Hartford, Connecticut 06106.

Delaware Tourism Office, 99 Kings Highway, Box 1401, Dover, Delaware 19903.

Florida Division of Tourism, 410 Collins Building, Tallahassee, Florida 32301.

Georgia Department of Industry & Trade, Tourist Division, P.O. Box 1776, Atlanta, Georgia 30301.

Idaho Travel Council, Statehouse, Boise, Idaho 83720.

Louisiana—Office of Tourism, Box 94291, Baton Rouge, Louisiana 70804-9291.

Maine Publicity Bureau, 97 Winthrop Street, Hallowell, Maine 04347.

Massachusetts Department of Commerce and Development, Division of Tourism, 100 Cambridge Street, Boston, Massachusetts 02202.

Michigan Travel Bureau, Department of Commerce, Post Office Box 30226, Lansing, Michigan 48909.

Minnesota Office of Tourism, 419 N. Robert Street, St. Paul, Minnesota 55101.

Montana Promotion Division, Department of Commerce, 1424 Ninth Avenue, Helena, Montana 59620.

Nevada Commission on Tourism, Capitol Complex, Carson City, Nevada 89710.

New Hampshire Vacations, Post Office Box 856, Concord, New Hampshire 03301.

New Jersey Division of Travel & Tourism, CN-826, Trenton, New Jersey 08625.

New Mexico Tourism and Travel Division, Bataan Memorial Building, Santa Fe, New Mexico 87503.

New York State Department of Commerce, Division of Tourism, 1 Commerce Plaza, Albany, New York 12245.

Oregon Economic Development Department, Tourism Division, 595 Cottage Street N.E., Salem, Oregon 97310.

Pennsylvania Bureau of Travel Development, Department of Commerce, 416 Forum Building, Harrisbug, Pennsylvania 17120.

Utah Travel Council, Council Hall, Capitol Hill, Salt Lake City, Utah 84114.

Vermont Travel Division, 134 State Street, Montpelier, Vermont 05602.

Washington State Tourism Development Division, Department of Commerce and Economic Development, 101 General Administration Building, Olympia, Washington 98504.

Wisconsin Division of Tourism, Post Office Box 7606, Madison, Wisconsin 53707.

Wyoming Travel Commission, Frank Norris Jr. Travel Center, Cheyenne, Wyoming 82002.

Some European Tourist Offices in the Unites States

Belgian Tourist Office, 745 Fifth Ave., New York, New York 10151.

Danish Tourist Board, 8929 Wilshire Blvd., Beverly Hills, California 90211.

Finnish Tourist Board, 655 Third Ave., New York, New York 10017.

French Government Tourist Office, 9401 Wilshire Blvd., Beverly Hills, California 90212.

Italian Government Travel Office, 360 Post St., San Francisco, California 94108.

Luxembourg National Tourist Office, 801 Second Ave., New York, New York 10017.

Norwegian Tourist Board, 655 Third Ave., New York, New York 10017.

Swiss National Tourist Office, 608 Fifth Avenue, New York, New York 10020 and 250 Stockton St., San Francisco, California 94108.

Most of these offices have (free) 800 numbers which change from time to time, as do the personnel.

Selected Bibliography

Reference Books

Atlas of the World. Washington, D.C.: National Geographic Society, 1981.

Bartlett, John. *Familiar Quotations.* Boston: Little Brown, 1980.

Burack, Sylvia K., ed. *The Writer's Handbook.* Boston: The Writer, 1987.

Duboff, Leonard D. *The Law (in Plain English) for Writers.* Seattle: Madrona Publishers, 1987.

Follett, W. *Modern American Usage.* New York: Hill & Wang, 1966.

Gonzales, Laurence. *Computers for Writers.* New York: Ballantine, 1986.

Hotel & Motel Red Book. New York: American Hotel Association Directory Corporation. (Yearly)

Jordan, Lewis, ed. *The New York Times Manual of Style and Usage.* New York: New York Times Books, 1976.

Roget's International Thesaurus. New York: Thomas Crowell, 1977.

Roget's Thesaurus in Dictionary Form. New York: G. P. Putnam's Sons, 1978.

Webster's New Geographical Dictionary. Springfield, Mass.: Merriam-Webster, 1984.

Webster's Ninth New Collegiate Dictionary. 9th ed. Springfield, Mass.: Merriam-Webster, 1987.

Zinsser, William. *On Writing Well: An Informal Guide to Writing Nonfiction.* 3rd ed. New York: Harper & Row, 1985.

Magazines & Newsletters

Freelancer's Newsletter. 307 Westlake Dr., Austin, TX 78746.

Freelance Writer's Report. Fort Lauderdale, Fla.: Cassell Communications Inc.

Markets Abroad. Michael Sedge & Associates, 2460 Lexington Dr., Owosso, Mich. 48867. (Quarterly)

Photoletter. Osceola, Wisconsin 54020.

Publisher's Weekly. 1180 Ave. of the Americas, New York 10036.

Travel Writer's Markets. Elaine O'Gara, ed. Berkeley, Calif.: Winterbourne Press. (Yearly)

Travelwriter Marketletter. Plaza Hotel, 5th Ave. and 59th St., New York, NY 10019.

The Writer. 8 Arlington St., Boston, MA 02116.

Writer's Digest. 22 E. 12th St., Cincinnati, OH 45210.

Marketing

Adams, Jane. *How to Sell What You Write.* New York: G. P. Putnam's Sons, 1984.

Casewit, Curtis. *Freelance Writing: Advice From the Pros.* New York: Collier/Macmillan, revised edition, 1985.

Cassill, Kay. *The Complete Handbook for Freelance Writers.* Cincinnati, Ohio: Writer's Digest, 1982.

Editor & Publisher Yearbook. New York: Editor & Publisher. (Yearly)

Engh, Rohn. *Sell & Re-Sell Your Photos.* Cincinnati, Ohio: Writer's Digest, 1981, 1985.

Literary Market Place. New York: R. R. Bowker. (Yearly)

Magazine Market Place. New York: R. R. Bowker. (Yearly)

Meyer, Carol. *The Writer's Survival Manual.* New York: Bantam, 1984.

Sedge, Michael. *How to Double Your Income Through Foreign & Reprint Sales.* Michigan: Michael Sedge & Associates, 1987.

Writers and Artists Yearbook. Cincinnati, Ohio: Writer's Digest. (Yearly)

Writer's Market. Cincinnati, Ohio: Writer's Digest. (Yearly)

The Writing Business. New York: Poets & Writers, 1985.

Index